From Dude to L_
Essential Survival Guide for First-Time Fathers

Ultimate Pregnancy Guide for Men to Provide Stellar Support, Enjoy Nights of 'Zzz's and Ease, Stress-Free Pregnancy and Master Baby Development with Your Little MVP

Noah Smith

Legal Notice:
Copyright 2023 by Monica Fisher - All rights reserved.

This document is geared towards providing exact and reliable information regarding the topic and issue covered. The publication is sold on the idea that the publisher is not required to render an accounting, officially permitted, or otherwise, qualified services. If advice is necessary, legal, or professional, a practised individual in the profession should be ordered. From a Declaration of Principles which was accepted and approved equally by a Committee of the American Bar Association and a Committee of Publishers and Associations.

Disclaimer Notice:
The information herein is offered for informational purposes solely and is universal as so. The presentation of the information is without a contract or any type of guaranteed assurance. Readers acknowledge that the author is not engaging in the rendering of legal, financial, medical, or professional advice. Please consult a licensed professional before attempting any techniques outlined in this book. The trademarks that are used are without any consent, and the publication of the trademark is without permission or backing by the trademark owner. All trademarks and brands within this book are for clarifying purposes only and are the owned by the owners themselves, not affiliated with this document.

Table of Contents

Part 1: The First Trimester: From Conceiving to the First Few Months 6

    Introduction: Buckle Up, Dads! The Roller Coaster Ride of Parenthood Begins 7

Chapter 1: The Road to Parenthood: Conceiving and the Challenges Along the Way 10

    Baby-Making 101: Navigating the Hilarious Hurdles of Conception 11

    Infertility Woes: Surviving the Baby-Making Olympics 13

    Mission: Possible - Seeking Support and Exploring Baby-Making Options 16

    High-Tech Baby-Making: Embracing the Wild World of Reproductive Technologies 19

    Love, Laughter, and Baby-Making: Nurturing Your Relationship on the Conception Journey 21

Chapter 2: Transitioning into Fatherhood: Embracing the Adventure. 24

    From Dude to Dad: Embarking on the Adventure of a Lifetime 28

    Facing Fears and Finding Fun: How to Dad Like a Pro ... 31

Chapter 3: Understanding Pregnancy: The First Trimester 34

    Conception Chronicles: The Miracle of Life Begins 35

    Surviving the Hormonal Hurricane: Supporting Your Partner's Mood Swings 37

    Pregnancy Pizzazz: Nurturing the Bun in the Oven 40

    Comedy and Cravings: Handling the Hilarious Challenges of the First Trimester 42

Chapter 4: Navigating Prenatal Care: The First Trimester .. 45

Doctor's Orders and Tests Galore: Surviving Prenatal Appointments Like a Champ 46

Pregnant Partner, Happy Life: Supporting Your Better Half's Well-being 48

Tag Team Parenthood: Building a Strong Partnership on the Baby Journey 50

Part 2: The Second Trimester: Preparing for Parenthood ... 53

Chapter 5: Creating a Safe and Nurturing Environment 54

The Nesting Chronicles: Transforming Your Space for Tiny Tornadoes 55

Safety First, Laughs Later: Childproofing Like a Pro 60

Chapter 6: Financial Planning for Parenthood 65

Diapers and Dollars: Managing Your Baby Budget with Style 66

Insurance, Investing, and Inevitable Expenses: Navigating the Money Maze 70

Chapter 7: The Journey to Labor and Delivery: The Second Trimester 75

Cravings, Contractions, and Craziness: Supporting Your Partner through the Adventure 76

The Birth Plan Chronicles: Making Joint Decisions and Surviving the Delivery Room Drama 80

The Labor Diaries: What to Expect When Your Partner Is Expecting 84

Part 3: The Third Trimester: Mastering Newborn Care 88

Chapter 8: The First Days with Your Newborn 89

From Delivery Room to Dadeville: Welcoming Your Little Rockstar with Open Arms 90

Alien or Adorable? Decoding Newborn Appearance and Behaviors 93

Newborn behavior 95

Hospital Hijinks: A Dad's Survival Guide to Navigating the Baby Bubble 97

Chapter 9: Diaper Duty and Baby Basics 99

Diaper Disasters and Hilarious Hazards: Conquering the Art of Diaper Changing 100

Feeding Frenzy: Breast, Bottle, and the Great Solids Showdown 104

Splish Splash, Baby Bash: Grooming Your Little One with Finesse 107

Chapter 10: Soothing Techniques and Sleep Strategies .. 111

Cry Me a River: Dad's Guide to Taming the Tiny Tears 112

Sleep or Sigh? Mastering the Art of Slumber for Your Baby (and Yourself) 115

Dreamland Delights: Snooze Safely and Survive the SIDS Scare 118

Conclusion: Mission Accomplished? Reflecting on Your Epic Journey as a First-Time Father 122

From Rookie to Rockstar: Celebrating Your Dad Superpowers 123

Parenthood Unplugged: Embracing the Hilarious Hiccups and Heartwarming Moments 124

Part 1: The First Trimester: From Conceiving to the First Few Months

Introduction: Buckle Up, Dads! The Roller Coaster Ride of Parenthood Begins

Becoming a father is an amazing feeling and a long journey that has no end. So, you need to man up because, from the moment you first find out you're going to be a dad, your life is about to take a wild and extraordinary turn. This book, "From Dude to Dad," is your guidebook, your compass, and your cheering squad as you navigate the uncharted territories of fatherhood.

I know you might be feeling a mix of excitement, anticipation, and perhaps even a touch of nerves. Be rest assured, you're not alone. Every father-to-be has embarked on this adventure with a mix of emotions, and it's perfectly natural. Becoming a dad is a transformative experience, one that will test your limits, challenge your preconceptions, and fill your heart with a love you never knew existed.

In the pages that follow, we'll embark on a journey together, exploring each stage of the incredible transformation from a regular dude to a devoted and confident dad. We'll dive headfirst into the roller coaster ride of pregnancy, embracing the joys, fears, and unexpected twists that lie ahead. From the exhilaration of conception to the thrill of holding your newborn in your arms, we'll be your trusted companion, providing guidance, insights, and a healthy dose of humor along the way.

Just as pregnancy trimesters are three, this book is divided into three parts to enable you to understand the different stages of fatherhood. But more importantly, you have to focus on your wife's condition. You must assume your duty from conception by looking after your spouse and your unborn baby. So, what you will be reading in the subsequent paragraph is the breakdown of what you should expect at each, your role, and how to handle them.

Part 1: The First Trimester: From Conceiving to the First Few Months, will take you through the early stages of this awe-inspiring journey. We'll tackle the challenges of conception, support you through the hormonal hurricane of the first trimester, and empower you to navigate prenatal care like a champ. Together, we'll forge a strong partnership with your partner, laying a solid foundation for the adventure ahead.

Part 2: The Second Trimester: Preparing for Parenthood will guide you as you transform your environment into a safe haven for your little one. We'll explore the financial aspects of parenthood, ensuring you're equipped to navigate the money maze with confidence. With insights into the journey to labor and delivery, you'll be prepared to be your partner's rock and cheerleader throughout the exhilarating and unpredictable ride.

Part 3: The Third Trimester: Mastering Newborn Care is where we dive headfirst into the beautiful chaos of life with your newborn. From the first magical days together to mastering diaper duty, feeding frenzies, and soothing techniques, we'll equip you with the knowledge and skills to embrace the challenges and joys of early fatherhood.

Throughout this book, we'll celebrate your journey, highlighting your unique superpowers as a dad and uncovering the hilarity and heartwarming moments that make fatherhood truly extraordinary. You'll discover that, although it may sometimes feel like a whirlwind, this adventure is filled with boundless love, personal growth, and a profound connection with your child.

So, buckle up, dads! Together, we'll navigate the roller coaster ride of parenthood, embracing the unexpected, and emerging as confident, loving, and superhero dads. Let's embark on this incredible adventure and make lasting memories as we journey from dude to dad.

Good luck!

Chapter 1: The Road to Parenthood: Conceiving and the Challenges Along the Way

When it comes to love and life, there's an extraordinary adventure that surpasses all others, and that is obviously the remarkable journey of parenthood. It's a voyage where dreams are shared, and love knows no bounds, as two souls unite with the desire to bring a new life into this world. From the moment hope takes root, the path to parenthood unfolds, filled with a whirlwind of emotions, challenges, and moments of triumph that shape who we are. While we often hear about this journey from a mother's point of view, it's time we shed light on the unique perspective of fathers—a perspective that's filled with anticipation, vulnerability, and unwavering support.

In this chapter, I will be discussing the profound tale of men embracing the miracle of life, facing the obstacles that come our way, and ultimately discovering the transformative power of becoming a father.

Baby-Making 101: Navigating the Hilarious Hurdles of Conception

Embarking on the journey of starting a family can be an exciting and sometimes comical adventure. From the perspective of a father-to-be, the process of conception often involves navigating a series of hilarious hurdles. In this chapter, I will be delving into the world of baby-making from a father's point of view, highlighting the amusing aspects and sharing some relatable anecdotes along the way.

- Timing Is Everything: When it comes to baby-making, timing plays a crucial role. As a father, you quickly realize that you and your partner are now operating on a whole new schedule, meticulously tracking ovulation cycles and eagerly awaiting the "perfect" moment to try for a baby. This process can often lead to amusing situations, like finding yourself discreetly excusing yourself from social gatherings to ensure you don't miss that window of opportunity.

- The Art of Seduction: Conception can turn even the most stoic individuals into self-proclaimed experts in the art of seduction. Suddenly, everything becomes a potential aphrodisiac, from candles and romantic music to silk sheets and provocative lingerie. As a father, you'll find yourself embracing your inner Casanova, attempting to create the ideal ambiance for that special encounter, all in the name of baby-making.

- The Science of It All: Conception is, undeniably, a scientific process, but that doesn't mean it can't be hilarious. As a father-to-be, you may find yourself thrust into a world of acronyms and jargon like TTC (Trying to Conceive), BBT (Basal Body Temperature), and OPK (Ovulation Predictor Kits). Embracing these terms and their associated rituals can lead to some amusing moments, whether it's fumbling with a thermometer or deciphering the cryptic symbols on an ovulation test.

- Overthinking, Overanalyzing: The journey to conception can sometimes turn even the most laid-back individuals into overthinking experts. Suddenly, every minor change in your partner's body becomes a potential sign of pregnancy, leading to countless humorous scenarios where even the most innocuous symptoms are blown out of proportion. As a father, it's important to find humor in these moments and provide support, even when the alarm is raised over a sudden craving for pickles and ice cream.

- The Unexpected Surprises: Just when you think you have the whole baby-making process figured out, life throws you a curveball. From uncooperative pets who seem to sense the change in the air to well-meaning friends and family members who offer unsolicited advice, there's no shortage of unexpected surprises on this journey. Embrace the chaos, laugh it off, and remember that the road to conception is rarely a straight line.

Infertility Woes: Surviving the Baby-Making Olympics

Infertility can be a challenging and emotionally taxing journey for couples who are trying to conceive. It often feels like participating in a "baby-making Olympics" where there are numerous hurdles and setbacks along the way. However, with the right mindset, support, and resources, you can navigate this difficult path and increase your chances of having a baby. To survive this stage, I will like to share some strategies that will ease your journey through infertility.

Seek professional help: A lot of new couples make the mistake of surfing the internet for infertility remedies. That might not be fruitful. If you've been trying to conceive without success for a year (or six months if you're over 35), it's recommended to consult a fertility specialist. They can evaluate both partners, identify potential causes of infertility, and suggest appropriate treatments or interventions.

Educate yourself: In your journey of becoming a father, you will need to self-learn most of the time. However, you should learn about the reproductive process, common fertility issues, and available treatment options. Understanding the factors affecting fertility can help you make informed decisions and have more productive conversations with your healthcare provider.

Build a support system: Infertility can be isolating, but you're not alone. Connect with support groups, either in person or online, where you can share your experiences, emotions, and concerns with others who are going through similar struggles. Empathy, advice, and encouragement from others can provide significant emotional support.

Take care of your emotional well-being: Infertility can take a toll on your mental wellness. You should prioritize self-care and find healthy coping mechanisms. Consider activities like yoga, meditation, therapy, journaling, or engaging in hobbies that bring you joy and relaxation.

Communicate with your partner: Don't get it twisted; infertility can strain even the strongest relationships. Therefore, you need to maintain open and honest communication with your partner throughout the process. Share your feelings, fears, and hopes with each other, and work together as a team to navigate the challenges.

Prioritize your relationship: Trying to conceive can become all-consuming. So, you should not neglect your relationship with your partner. Set aside time for intimacy, romance, and fun activities that strengthen your bond. Doing this will remind you of the love and joy you share beyond the goal of having a baby. Do not allow this situation to make you a sad man.

Explore different treatment options: Fertility treatments can vary from lifestyle changes to medical interventions like assisted reproductive technologies (ART) such as in vitro fertilization (IVF), intrauterine insemination (IUI), or fertility medications. Work closely with your fertility specialist to determine the most suitable options for your situation.

Take breaks when needed: The infertility journey can be exhausting physically, emotionally, and financially. It's fine to take breaks or step back temporarily to focus on self-care and regroup.

Consider alternative paths to parenthood: There are numerous options to consider out there. So, if fertility treatments are unsuccessful or not viable options for you, you can explore alternative paths to parenthood such as adoption, surrogacy, or fostering. These options can provide fulfilling opportunities to become parents and create a loving family.

Stay hopeful and resilient: Infertility can be a long and challenging road, but it's important to remain hopeful and resilient. Remember that many couples have overcome infertility and successfully built their families. Stay positive, celebrate small victories, and keep your eyes on the ultimate goal of having a child.

My final note on this subsection is: Every journey is unique, and what works for others might not work for you. So, you should be patient, and kind to yourself, and don't hesitate to seek professional help and support along the way.

Mission: Possible - Seeking Support and Exploring Baby-Making Options

Starting a family can be an exciting and, sometimes, challenging endeavor. For individuals or couples seeking support and exploring baby-making options, there are various paths to consider. In this section, I will be providing you with an overview of different avenues, resources, and considerations to help make this mission possible.

Preconception Health: Before going deeper into the process of conceiving, you should prioritize preconception health. This involves maintaining a healthy lifestyle, addressing any existing medical conditions, and ensuring both partners are in optimal physical and mental health. Consulting with healthcare professionals can help identify potential risks, and offer guidance on nutrition, exercise, and lifestyle modifications.

Natural Conception: A lot of couples choose natural conception methods, which have to do with understanding the menstrual cycle and timing intercourse to match up the most fertile period. Tracking ovulation through methods like basal body temperature charting, cervical mucus monitoring, or ovulation prediction kits can boost the likelihood of successful pregnancy.

Fertility Testing and Treatment: When natural conception attempts are abortive, it might be helpful to opt for fertility testing to identify any underlying issues. Fertility specialists would conduct tests to assess factors such as hormone levels, semen analysis, ovarian reserve, or tubal patency. Based on the results, various fertility treatment options can be explored. These alternatives include:

a. Medications: Fertility medications such as Clomid or letrozole can be used to stimulate ovulation in women or improve sperm production in men.
b. Intrauterine Insemination (IUI): This procedure involves placing sperm directly into the uterus during the woman's fertile period to enhance the chances of fertilization.
c. In vitro fertilization (IVF): IVF is a more complex procedure where eggs are retrieved from the woman's ovaries, fertilized with sperm in a lab, and then transferred to the uterus.
d. Donor Gametes: In cases of severe infertility, donor eggs or sperm can be used to achieve pregnancy.
e. Surrogacy: Surrogacy involves another woman carrying the pregnancy on behalf of the intended parents. This option might be suitable for those who are unable to carry a pregnancy themselves.

Adoption: For individuals or couples who are unable to conceive or prefer not to pursue fertility treatments, adoption provides a wonderful opportunity to expand their family. Adoption agencies and organizations can guide prospective parents through the process, including home studies, legal requirements, and matching with a child.

Emotional and Psychological Support: Parenthood can potentially bring about a range of emotions. Therefore, you might be required to seek emotional support from loved ones, join support groups, or consider counseling to navigate the ups and downs of the process.

There are various resources available, including online forums, therapists, and support organizations specializing in fertility or adoption.

Financial Considerations: Do you know that exploring baby-making options often comes with financial implications? So, it's important to assess the costs associated with fertility treatments, adoption fees, or surrogacy arrangements. Researching insurance coverage, grants, loans, or employer assistance programs can provide financial relief and make the process more feasible.

High-Tech Baby-Making: Embracing the Wild World of Reproductive Technologies

In recent years, advancements in reproductive technologies have revolutionized the way we approach conception and pregnancy. From in vitro fertilization (IVF) to genetic testing and embryo selection, the realm of assisted reproduction has witnessed remarkable progress. Now, let's explore the fascinating world of high-tech baby-making and delves into the various technologies that are reshaping the future of human reproduction.

In Vitro Fertilization (IVF): Opening Doors to Parenthood In vitro fertilization has long been at the forefront of assisted reproductive technologies. IVF enables couples facing infertility or genetic challenges to conceive by combining eggs and sperm outside the body in a laboratory setting. With the ability to select the healthiest embryos for implantation, IVF offers new hope to couples seeking to start a family.

Preimplantation Genetic Testing (PGT): Paving the Way for Healthy Offspring PGT has emerged as a powerful tool in the world of reproductive technologies. It allows for the screening of embryos to identify genetic abnormalities or chromosomal disorders before implantation. By ensuring the transfer of healthy embryos, PGT minimizes the risk of passing on inherited diseases, significantly increasing the chances of a successful pregnancy.

Gamete and Embryo Cryopreservation: Preserving Future Possibilities Cryopreservation of eggs, sperm, and embryos has become a game-changer in reproductive technologies. By freezing and storing reproductive cells, individuals can preserve their fertility for later use, even if they are not ready to have children or are facing medical treatments that may impact their fertility. Cryopreservation offers newfound freedom and flexibility for family planning.

Surrogacy: Expanding the Boundaries of Parenthood
Surrogacy has gained popularity as a viable option for individuals or couples unable to carry a pregnancy to term. With the help of a gestational surrogate, intended parents can experience the joy of biological parenthood. High-tech advancements, such as in vitro fertilization and genetic testing, have further enhanced the success rates and safety of surrogacy arrangements.

Mitochondrial Replacement Therapy (MRT): Mitigating Genetic Disorders
Mitochondrial diseases, caused by genetic mutations in the mitochondria, can have severe implications for individuals and their offspring. MRT offers a groundbreaking solution by replacing defective mitochondria with healthy ones from a donor. This technique holds immense promise for preventing the transmission of mitochondrial disorders and improving the health outcomes of future generations.

Artificial Wombs: Redefining the Concept of Pregnancy
While still in the experimental stages, artificial wombs are a revolutionary concept in reproductive technologies. These devices aim to provide a nurturing environment for gestating fetuses outside the human body. Artificial wombs could potentially offer a lifeline for premature babies or those born with complications, redefining our understanding of pregnancy and childbirth.

Genetic Engineering and Designer Babies: Ethical Considerations Advancements in genetic engineering technologies, such as CRISPR-Cas9, have sparked debates around the concept of "designer babies." The ability to edit specific genes raises ethical concerns about the potential for creating genetically modified humans. Society grapples with the delicate balance between the pursuit of genetic enhancement and the preservation of human diversity.

Love, Laughter, and Baby-Making: Nurturing Your Relationship on the Conception Journey
The journey toward starting a family comes with mixed emotions. While the primary focus often revolves around conception and fertility, it's crucial not to overlook the importance of nurturing your relationship during this time. Love, laughter, and a strong bond between partners can significantly contribute to a positive conception journey. In this last section, I would love to share some amazing details on how to foster love, maintain laughter, and strengthen your relationship while navigating the path toward creating a new life.

Here is a list of what you should focus on:

Prioritize Emotional Connection: Conceiving a baby involves both physical and emotional aspects. During this time, you must prioritize emotional connection with your partner. Engage in open and honest communication, expressing your desires, fears, and expectations. Share your dreams and aspirations for the future, allowing your relationship to deepen and grow.

Take the time to truly listen and understand each other, creating a safe and supportive space for both of you.

Embrace Laughter and Joy: Laughter is often called the best medicine, and it holds in the realm of relationships too. Infuse your journey with joy, playfulness, and laughter. Find moments to let go of stress and enjoy each other's company. Engage in activities that make you both laugh, such as watching funny movies, sharing jokes, or engaging in light-hearted games. Laughter not only strengthens your bond but also reduces stress and creates a positive atmosphere conducive to conception.

Create Rituals of Connection: Amidst the appointments, tests, and ovulation cycles, it's easy to get caught up in the mechanics of baby-making. To nurture your relationship, establish rituals of connection.

Set aside quality time for each other, free from distractions. Plan date nights, romantic getaways, or even simple walks in nature where you can reconnect and deepen your intimacy. These rituals remind you of the love and passion that brought you together in the first place.

Support Each Other's Emotional Well-being: Conception journeys can be emotionally challenging, especially if there are obstacles or setbacks along the way. It's crucial to support each other's emotional well-being. Be empathetic and understanding, acknowledging the rollercoaster of emotions that both of you may experience.

Offer a shoulder to lean on, be a listening ear, and provide encouragement when needed. By nurturing each other's emotional health, you create a strong foundation for the journey ahead.

Celebrate Milestones and Victories: Every step closer to conception is a milestone worth celebrating. Regardless of the outcome, acknowledge and celebrate each small victory along the way. Whether it's a positive ovulation test, a successful fertility treatment, or simply maintaining a positive mindset, take the time to recognize your accomplishments as a couple. This reinforces your commitment to the journey and fosters a sense of togetherness.

Practice Self-Care as a Couple: Self-care is not limited to individuals; it can also be a shared experience. Find ways to practice self-care as a couple. Doing this will give room for both partners to recharge and rejuvenate. Engage in activities that bring you joy, relaxation, and peace, whether it's a couple's massage, a weekend getaway, or simply enjoying a quiet evening at home. By taking care of yourselves individually and as a couple, you create a nurturing environment for your relationship to thrive.

Chapter 2: Transitioning into Fatherhood: Embracing the Adventure.

Fatherhood is a forever adventure, and nobody is born to become a father. But I can assure you that you can do it well. All it takes is intentionality. Be willing to take responsibility. Sooner or later, you have everything figured out.

Without mincing words, transitioning into fatherhood has a myriad of cherishable feelings and emotions. However, it comes with its dark sides because nothing good comes with ease. Therefore, you must prepare your mind to embrace the adventure and its likely challenges.

In essence, I will be talking about the journey to fatherhood in this chapter and the fears, and how you can find fun through the adventure. But before I dive into the details, let me share an inspiring story of Ethan to fatherhood. I know you will have some lessons to grasp from his journey.

Here is the story:

Ethan had always been known for his adventurous spirit and zest for life. From climbing towering mountains to exploring deep forests, Ethan had seen it all. But little did he know that his greatest adventure was about to begin—a journey into fatherhood.
He was a passionate soul, filled with curiosity and an unwavering love for the unknown.

He had recently married his childhood sweetheart, Olivia, and they were eagerly expecting their first child. As the due date approached, Ethan's heart swelled with a mix of excitement and nervousness. He had climbed cliffs and faced fierce storms, but nothing compared to the overwhelming joy and responsibility of becoming a father.

The day finally arrived when Olivia gave birth to a beautiful baby girl named Lily. The moment Ethan held her tiny fingers in his hand, a surge of love rushed through him, dissolving any lingering doubts or fears. He knew from that very instant that his life had changed forever. His heart now beat for two—his adventures and the journey of fatherhood.

Ethan embraced the challenges of fatherhood with open arms. He was determined to be the best father he could be for Lily. Just as he had prepared for his daring expeditions, he dedicated himself to learning about parenthood. He devoured books, attended parenting classes, and sought advice from experienced fathers. Every obstacle that came his way was approached with the same spirit of adventure he had displayed in the great outdoors.

Fatherhood, Ethan discovered, was an incredible expedition filled with unexpected twists and turns. There were sleepless nights, diaper changes, and soothing cries that tested his endurance. But in those quiet moments, when Lily would gaze at him with her innocent eyes, Ethan felt an overwhelming sense of fulfillment that no mountain peak could ever provide.

As Lily grew, Ethan found himself rediscovering the world through her eyes. They embarked on countless adventures together, exploring their surroundings with childlike wonder. Ethan would take Lily to the park, where they would swing high into the sky, feeling the wind against their faces. They would build sandcastles on the beach, their laughter blending with the sound of crashing waves. And during rainy afternoons, they would dance in puddles, embracing the joy of simply being alive.

Through the ups and downs of fatherhood, Ethan learned that it wasn't about being a perfect parent; it was about being present, loving, and patient. He cherished every milestone, from Lily's first steps to her first words, knowing that he was witnessing the blossoming of a beautiful soul.
Fatherhood taught Ethan the true meaning of adventure. It wasn't just about scaling mountains or traversing treacherous paths—it was about guiding a young life, nurturing a spirit, and watching it flourish. It was about embracing the unknown, for every day brought new challenges and rewards.
Years passed, and Ethan watched proudly as Lily grew into a strong and independent young woman. She had inherited his love for adventure and embarked on her own expeditions, while always carrying the lessons her father had taught her. Together, they had created a bond that would withstand any storm, a bond forged through the shared adventure of fatherhood.

And so, as the sun set behind the familiar hills, Ethan sat with Lily by his side, reflecting on the journey they had taken together. At that moment, he knew that transitioning into fatherhood had been the greatest adventure of his life—one that had filled his heart with boundless love, unbreakable bonds, and memories that would forever resonate in their souls.

That's the story of Ethan and his daughter, Lily. Now, let's get into the real deal of this chapter.

From Dude to Dad: Embarking on the Adventure of a Lifetime

Becoming a father is a transformative journey that takes a man from the carefree days of being a "dude" to embracing the responsibilities and joys of fatherhood. This adventure is filled with incredible experiences, challenges, and personal growth that can change a man's life in profound ways. From late-night diaper changes to heartwarming first words, the transition from dude to dad is a remarkable chapter in a man's life. Are you ready to explore the adventure of a lifetime that awaits all soon-to-be fathers?

Embracing the Expectant Dad Mindset: The moment you discover that you're going to be a father, a whirlwind of emotions and thoughts ensues. This phase is an opportune time to prepare mentally and emotionally for the upcoming responsibilities. From educating oneself about prenatal care and childbirth to understanding the importance of emotional support, this is the foundation upon which the journey to fatherhood begins.

Supporting Your Partner: Pregnancy and childbirth can be challenging for mothers, both physically and emotionally. As a dad-to-be, providing unwavering support to your partner becomes a crucial role. From attending doctor's appointments to offering a listening ear and lending a helping hand, being there for your partner is an essential aspect of the adventure.

Preparing for the Arrival: Creating a safe and welcoming environment for your child is a significant step in the journey.

From setting up the nursery to babyproofing the house, the preparation phase allows dads to showcase their nurturing side and make practical arrangements to ensure their little one's comfort.

Embracing the Firsts: The arrival of your baby brings a cascade of first-time experiences that will leave a lasting imprint on your heart. From witnessing your child's first smile to celebrating milestones like rolling over, sitting up, and taking those first wobbly steps, every achievement becomes a cherished memory.

Building Strong Bonds: The relationship between a father and child is unique and transformative. From bonding through playtime, bedtime stories, and shared adventures, fathers play a vital role in their child's emotional development. Exploring ways to strengthen the father-child bond ensures a lifetime of love, trust, and companionship.

Overcoming Challenges: Fatherhood is not without its share of challenges. From sleepless nights to balancing work and family life, navigating the obstacles requires resilience and adaptability. Finding support networks, seeking advice, and learning from other experienced dads can help overcome these challenges and grow as a father.

Discovering New Perspectives: Becoming a father broadens your horizons and helps you see the world through a fresh set of eyes. The innocence, curiosity, and boundless imagination of your child remind you of the beauty in the simplest things.

From exploring nature to engaging in imaginative play, rediscovering the world through your child's perspective adds a new layer of wonder to your own life.

Embracing Personal Growth: Fatherhood is an opportunity for personal growth and self-discovery. The journey pushes you to develop patience, empathy, and selflessness. It challenges your preconceived notions and helps you redefine your priorities, teaching you valuable lessons that extend beyond fatherhood.

What I want you to take away from this subsection is that the transition from being a dude to a dad is a profound adventure that brings joy, challenges, personal growth, and countless unforgettable moments. Embracing this journey wholeheartedly allows you to step into the role of a father with enthusiasm and dedication. From nurturing your child's development to creating lasting memories, the adventure of a lifetime awaits you as a dad, offering you a chance to experience love, connection, and fulfillment like never before.

Facing Fears and Finding Fun: How to Dad Like a Pro

To be a father is a remarkable journey filled with countless joys, challenges, and yes, fears. From changing diapers to handling sleepless nights, dads often find themselves stepping into uncharted territory. However, with the right mindset and a dash of creativity, any dad can embrace the adventure of fatherhood and transform it into a fun-filled experience for both themselves and their children. In this subsection, I will share some valuable tips and tricks to help you face your fears head-on and unlock your inner superhero, all while creating unforgettable memories with your little ones.

1. Embrace Your Fears

Fear is a natural part of parenting, but it shouldn't hold you back. Identifying your fears and understanding their root causes is the first step to overcoming them. Whether it's changing a diaper for the first time or handling a crying baby, acknowledge your apprehensions and face them head-on. Don't forget that you're not alone, and every dad has been through similar experiences.

2. Educate Yourself

Knowledge is power, especially for new dads. Read books, attend parenting classes, and seek advice from experienced fathers. Learning about child development, safety precautions, and effective parenting techniques will boost your confidence and equip you with the skills needed to navigate the challenges that come your way.

3. Embrace Playfulness

Children are masters of finding fun in the simplest of things, and dads can learn a lot from their sense of playfulness. Embrace your inner child and let go of inhibitions. Engage in imaginative play, build forts, have tickle fights, or create silly dance routines together. Being a dad doesn't mean you have to be serious all the time—let loose and have fun!

4. Create Rituals and Traditions

Rituals and traditions are not only special but also provide a sense of security for children. Establishing regular routines, such as reading bedtime stories or having a weekly family game night, creates a foundation of trust and togetherness. These rituals will not only make memories but also help you connect with your children on a deeper level.

5. Step Outside Your Comfort Zone

As a dad, it's important to encourage your children to explore new experiences. However, this means stepping out of your own comfort zone too. Try new activities together—whether it's learning to ride a bike, baking cookies, or even attempting a science experiment. By facing your own fears and trying new things alongside your children, you'll inspire them to be courageous and curious individuals.

6. Celebrate Mistakes and Learn Together

Parenting is a continuous learning process, and making mistakes is inevitable. Instead of being hard on yourself, celebrate your imperfections and turn them into opportunities for growth. Learn from your mistakes and involve your children in the process.

Teach them that setbacks are a part of life and that it's okay to make errors. By doing so, you'll foster resilience and a growth mindset in your children.

The bottom line is being a dad is an adventure that requires courage, resilience, and a sprinkle of fun. By embracing your fears, expanding your knowledge, and immersing yourself in playfulness, you can navigate the challenges of fatherhood like a pro. You should create lasting memories with your children, step out of your comfort zone, and learn from every experience. Bear in mind that you are not just a dad—you're a superhero in the eyes of your children. So, gear up, face your fears, and embark on a remarkable journey of fatherhood that will leave an indelible mark on both your children's lives and yours.

Chapter 3: Understanding Pregnancy: The First Trimester

If you're a first-time dad, you need to pay attention to certain things about pregnancy, especially when your partner is in the first trimester. In this chapter, I will walk you through 4 subsections that will equip you with the right information for the first trimester. Also, you learn what to do at different times and how to handle most of the situations. I guess you're ready for this information because it is transformational.

If you are set, let's get into the details.

Conception Chronicles: The Miracle of Life Begins

Conception is an extraordinary event that marks the beginning of new life. While it is often portrayed as solely a woman's experience, it's important to recognize and celebrate the role men play in this miraculous journey. This chapter delves into the awe-inspiring world of conception from a men's point of view, exploring the emotional, physical, and psychological aspects of this life-changing process.

So, let's into some of the amazing details of this subsection.

The Wonder of Life's Creation
From the moment of conception, you should become an active participant in the creation of life. It's a breathtaking realization that your genetic material merges with your partner's, laying the foundation for a unique and individual being. Witnessing this miracle can evoke a profound sense of awe, appreciation, and responsibility.

Emotional Rollercoaster
The journey to conception can be an emotional rollercoaster for you as a man. It's a time filled with anticipation, excitement, and, at times, anxiety. The desire to become a father, coupled with the uncertainties and challenges of fertility, can evoke a wide range of emotions. You might experience a deep longing, hopefulness, and even moments of vulnerability as you embark on this transformative path.

Supporting Your Partner

Conception is a shared journey, and as a man, supporting your partner is crucial during this time. Understanding her physical and emotional needs, offering a listening ear, and being actively involved in the process can strengthen the bond between you. Accompanying her to doctor's appointments, educating yourself about fertility, and participating in decisions regarding fertility treatments are some ways to show your support.

The Importance of Health

Your health, as a man, plays a vital role in conception. Maintaining a healthy lifestyle, including a balanced diet, regular exercise, and managing stress, can contribute to optimal reproductive health. You should also avoid harmful substances like tobacco and excessive alcohol consumption. By prioritizing your well-being, you are actively investing in the future well-being of your potential child.

Fertility Challenges and Seeking Help

Sometimes, the path to conception may present challenges. Infertility can affect both men and women and seeking professional help is crucial. Understanding that infertility is not a reflection of masculinity but rather a medical condition can help overcome any stigma or shame associated with the diagnosis. Seeking assistance from fertility specialists can provide invaluable guidance, support, and potential solutions.

Bonding with Your Unborn Child

As conception progresses and pregnancy ensues, you can begin to form a connection with your unborn child.

Engaging in activities like reading to the baby, talking or singing to the growing belly, and attending prenatal classes together can foster a sense of closeness and involvement. Embracing this unique opportunity to connect with the child before birth can strengthen the bond between father and child.

Preparing for Fatherhood
Conception is not just the beginning of life but also the initiation of a man's journey into fatherhood. Taking time to prepare mentally, emotionally, and practically for this role is essential. Educate yourself about parenting, and discuss your expectations with your partner. In essence, engaging in open communication can contribute to a smoother transition into fatherhood. Ensure you build a support network of fellow fathers or seek guidance from experienced parents; this can also be beneficial.

Surviving the Hormonal Hurricane: Supporting Your Partner's Mood Swings
Navigating the ups and downs of mood swings can be challenging, both for the person experiencing them and their partner. Hormonal fluctuations can significantly impact your partner's emotions, causing mood swings that may seem unpredictable and intense. In this subsection, I will be talking about how partners can provide understanding, support, and stability during these hormonal hurricanes, fostering a stronger and more compassionate relationship.

Here are a few things you can do to help the situation:

Educate Yourself
Understanding the hormonal changes your partner is going through is the first step in offering support. Research and learn about the hormones involved, such as estrogen and progesterone, and how they can affect mood and emotions. Recognize that these changes are a natural part of the menstrual cycle, pregnancy, or menopause, and not something your partner can control.

Communicate with Empathy
Open and empathetic communication is vital when supporting a partner experiencing mood swings. Create a safe space where they feel comfortable expressing their emotions without judgment. Be patient, listen actively, and validate their feelings. You should bear in mind that it's not about finding solutions right away but providing a compassionate presence and understanding.

Be Mindful of Triggers
Identify potential triggers that may intensify mood swings and try to minimize them. These triggers can be different for everyone but may include stress, fatigue, certain foods, or specific situations. By being aware of these triggers, you can help create a more harmonious environment and reduce unnecessary emotional distress.

Practice Self-Care
Taking care of yourself is essential when supporting a partner through hormonal mood swings.

It's important to maintain your own emotional well-being, so you can be a stable source of support. Engage in activities that recharge you, seek support from friends or family, and consider talking to a therapist if needed. You also need to acknowledge the fact that self-care is not selfish but necessary for both of you.

Offer Practical Support
Practical gestures of support can go a long way in alleviating stress during mood swings. Help with household chores, prepare meals, or offer to take care of any tasks that may feel overwhelming for your partner. By lightening their load, you create a sense of relief and allow them to focus on self-care and managing their emotions.

Explore Coping Mechanisms Together
Discovering effective coping mechanisms can be a joint effort. Encourage your partner to explore activities that help regulate their emotions, such as exercise, meditation, journaling, or creative outlets. Accompany them in trying out new techniques, and finding what works best for them as a couple. Together, you can develop strategies to navigate the hormonal roller coaster.

Seek Professional Help if Needed
If the mood swings become overwhelming or significantly impact your partner's daily life, it may be beneficial to seek professional help. Encourage your partner to consult with their healthcare provider or a mental health professional who specializes in hormone-related mood disorders. Professional guidance can provide additional support and offer strategies tailored to your partner's specific needs.

Pregnancy Pizzazz: Nurturing the Bun in the Oven
Nurturing the "bun in the oven" involves taking care of both the physical and emotional well-being of the expectant mother. In this section, you will learn ways to embrace the journey of pregnancy and provide practical tips to ensure a healthy and vibrant experience for both the mother and the growing baby.

To nurture the "Bun in the oven," you should try the following activities:

Embrace Self-Care
Pregnancy is a time when self-care takes center stage. Encourage the expectant mother to prioritize her well-being by engaging in activities that promote relaxation and reduce stress. Gentle exercises, such as prenatal yoga or swimming, can help maintain physical fitness while providing a sense of calm. Pampering routines like prenatal massages or warm baths can also contribute to a nurturing self-care regimen.

Nourish with a Balanced Diet
A well-balanced diet is crucial for the health and development of both mother and baby. Encourage the intake of nutrient-rich foods, including fresh fruits and vegetables, whole grains, lean proteins, and healthy fats. Adequate hydration is also vital. Support your partner by participating in meal planning and preparation, ensuring she receives the necessary nutrients for a healthy pregnancy.

Attend Prenatal Care Appointments
I mentioned this briefly while discussing the ways you can help your pregnant partner through her mood swings. However, accompanying your partner to prenatal care appointments demonstrates your

involvement and support. These appointments provide essential medical guidance and allow healthcare professionals to monitor the progress of the pregnancy. They also offer an opportunity to ask questions, gain knowledge about the baby's development, and bond as expectant parents.

Encourage Open Communication
Pregnancy brings about a whirlwind of emotions. Encourage your partner to openly express her feelings, fears, and joys. Create a safe space for her to share her experiences, offering active and non-judgmental listening. By fostering open communication, you can navigate the emotional journey together and strengthen your bond as expectant parents.

Get Involved in Baby Preparation
Preparing for the arrival of a baby can be an exciting and fulfilling experience. Engage in activities such as setting up the nursery, assembling furniture, and choosing baby essentials together. Attend childbirth education classes as a couple to learn about labor, delivery, and newborn care. By actively participating in these preparations, you'll deepen your connection with the baby and enhance your sense of partnership.

Provide Physical Support
As the pregnancy progresses, the expectant mother's body undergoes significant changes. Offer physical support by helping with tasks that may become more challenging, such as bending down to pick up objects or tying shoelaces. Offer foot rubs, back massages, or gentle stretches to alleviate discomfort. Showing your care through these gestures can make a significant difference in her comfort and well-being.

Celebrate Milestones

Celebrate and cherish the milestones of pregnancy. Document the journey by taking photographs, creating a pregnancy journal, or recording special moments. Plan small surprises or gestures to commemorate important events like the baby's first kicks or ultrasounds. By celebrating these milestones together, you create lasting memories and reinforce the joyous nature of pregnancy.

Comedy and Cravings: Handling the Hilarious Challenges of the First Trimester

The first trimester of pregnancy is a roller coaster ride filled with unique challenges and surprises. Amidst the physical changes and emotional ups and downs, expectant mothers often encounter moments of unexpected humor and intense cravings. In this subsection, I will share the funny side of the first trimester with you and provide tips for handling the delightful comedy and cravings that come along with it. Check out the tips!

The Comedy of Hormones

During the first trimester, hormonal changes can wreak havoc on a woman's emotions and reactions. It's not uncommon for expectant mothers to experience mood swings that oscillate between laughter and tears. The simplest things can suddenly become the funniest, leading to bouts of uncontrollable giggles. Embrace the humor and enjoy these spontaneous moments of comedy, both for you and the expectant mother.

Unpredictable Cravings

Cravings are infamous during pregnancy, especially in the first trimester. Suddenly, the expectant mother may have intense and peculiar desires for specific foods, combinations, or even non-edible items. From pickles and ice cream to the odd pairing of peanut butter and pickles, cravings can be both amusing and bewildering. Embrace the journey by accommodating these cravings when possible, as long as they align with a healthy diet.

Exploring Culinary Adventures

Pregnancy cravings often lead to culinary adventures and unusual food combinations. Encourage the expectant mother to explore her cravings while maintaining a balanced diet. Get creative in the kitchen by experimenting with new recipes or finding healthier alternatives to fulfill those cravings.
Approach the process with an open mind and a sense of humor, knowing that these culinary adventures are part of the delightful journey.

Sharing the Laughter

The comedic moments of the first trimester are meant to be shared and enjoyed together. Laughing together strengthens the bond between expectant parents and creates lasting memories. Share funny stories or moments with family and friends, providing a lighthearted perspective on the joys and challenges of pregnancy. Laughter not only lightens the mood but also eases any stress or anxieties along the way.

Finding Comfort

While the first trimester can be humorous, it's also important to address any discomfort or challenges that may arise.

Encourage the expectant mother to communicate her needs and concerns openly. Provide physical and emotional support, whether it's helping with household chores, offering a foot rub, or simply being a compassionate listener. Creating a comfortable and nurturing environment will help alleviate any difficulties and enhance the overall pregnancy experience.

We have come to the end of this chapter, I guess you must be looking forward to more amazing information in the next chapter. Keep on reading through the pages!

Chapter 4: Navigating Prenatal Care: The First Trimester

The journey of the usual nine months of pregnancy comes with a lot of commitments. And navigating through prenatal care is not child's play, especially if you are a first-time dad. But you need not to fret. I have prepared all you need to know and do in this chapter. From regular visits to the healthcare to the support you need to show to the mother of your unborn kids to building a formidable partnership with your pregnant partner, I can assure you that you will scale through this phase. However, it might be a little hectic and demanding on your part at the beginning.

Now, let's check out the content of this chapter.

Doctor's Orders and Tests Galore: Surviving Prenatal Appointments Like a Champ

"Doctor's Orders and Tests Galore: Surviving Prenatal Appointments like a Champ" refers to the experience of accompanying one's partner to prenatal appointments during pregnancy. These appointments are important for monitoring the health and progress of both the mother and the baby. As a man, being supportive and actively involved in these appointments can make a positive difference in the pregnancy journey.

The phrase "Doctor's Orders" indicates that the medical professional provides instructions and recommendations regarding the mother's health, prenatal care, and any necessary tests. These orders are crucial for ensuring a healthy pregnancy and addressing any potential complications. By following these instructions, you are contributing to the well-being of your partner and the unborn child.

"Tests Galore" implies that there are numerous medical examinations and screenings involved in prenatal care. These tests are performed to assess the baby's growth, monitor the mother's health, and identify any potential risks or abnormalities. You must understand the purpose of these tests and their significance in ensuring a healthy pregnancy.

To "Survive Prenatal Appointments like a Champ" means to approach these appointments with a positive attitude, actively engage in the process, and provide support to your pregnant partner.

It could mean being present during appointments, asking questions, and participating in discussions with the doctor. By doing so, you are demonstrating your commitment, showing care for your partner's well-being, and strengthening the bond between you and the expectant mother as you both prepare for parenthood.

In essence, the focus of this subsection is to encourage you to actively participate in prenatal appointments, follow the doctor's instructions, and be supportive throughout the pregnancy journey. By doing this, you are contributing to a healthier and more positive experience for your partner and the baby.

Pregnant Partner, Happy Life: Supporting Your Better Half's Well-being

"Pregnant Partner, Happy Life: Supporting Your Better Half's Well-being" refers to the importance of providing support and care to your pregnant partner. The well-being of both the pregnant woman and the relationship can be greatly enhanced by actively engaging in various ways during this transformative time.

The phrase "Pregnant Partner" emphasizes the central focus of this subsection on the woman who is carrying the baby. Recognizing her as a partner acknowledges the shared responsibility and commitment to the pregnancy journey. It emphasizes the significance of actively supporting her physical and emotional well-being.

"Happy Life" suggests that supporting your pregnant partner contributes to a positive and fulfilling life for both individuals. By understanding and empathizing with the physical and emotional changes she experiences, you are fostering an environment of happiness and support throughout the pregnancy.

In this section as well, the aim is to emphasize the importance of "Supporting Your Better Half's Well-being." This includes being attentive to her needs, both practical and emotional. Practical support may involve assisting with household chores, accompanying her to prenatal appointments, or helping with childcare responsibilities.

Emotional support encompasses actively listening, offering encouragement, and being patient and understanding during moments of mood swings or discomfort.

By actively participating in the pregnancy journey, you should foster a deeper connection with your partner. This involvement can be demonstrated through engaging in open and honest communication, discussing plans for the future, and actively seeking information about pregnancy and childbirth.

Therefore, you must be actively involved in supporting your pregnant partners. By doing so, you are contributing to a happier, healthier, and more fulfilling life for both yourself and your partner. Supporting your better half's well-being can strengthen the bond between both of you and create a positive foundation for the upcoming challenges and joys of parenthood.

Tag Team Parenthood: Building a Strong Partnership on the Baby Journey

Embarking on the journey of parenthood is an exciting and transformative experience for couples. It requires teamwork, communication, and a strong partnership to navigate the joys and challenges that come with raising a child. In this last subsection, I will walk you through the concept of tag team parenthood, where both parents work together as a cohesive unit, supporting each other and building a strong foundation for their baby's future. So, here are a few points you need to pay attention to and actively involve in while building a strong partnership with the expectant mother on the baby journey:

Embrace Shared Responsibilities
Tag team parenthood begins with a mindset of shared responsibilities. Both parents play a vital role in caring for the baby, and it's important to distribute tasks and duties equitably. From diaper changes to late-night feedings, dividing responsibilities allows each partner to have their own designated roles while maintaining a sense of balance and fairness.

Open and Effective Communication
Clear and open communication is the cornerstone of a successful parenting partnership. Discussing expectations, concerns, and challenges openly can help avoid misunderstandings and foster a supportive environment. Regularly check in with each other, share your thoughts, and actively listen to your partner's perspective. This ensures that both parents are on the same page and can work together towards common goals.

Support Each Other's Well-being
Parenting can be physically and emotionally demanding, so it's crucial to prioritize each other's well-being. Take turns giving each other breaks and opportunities for self-care. Support your partner's hobbies, interests, and personal time, as it rejuvenates their spirit and enhances their ability to be fully present as parents. By nurturing each other, you create a harmonious environment for both yourselves and your baby.

Teamwork in Decision-Making
Making decisions together strengthens your partnership and helps build trust. From choosing a pediatrician to deciding on parenting philosophies, involve each other in the decision-making process. Respect each other's opinions, discuss options, and find compromises that align with your shared values. This approach not only fosters unity but also creates a sense of ownership and joint responsibility for the well-being of your child.

Celebrate Milestones and Achievements
Parenting is a journey filled with milestones, big and small. Celebrate each achievement as a team, whether it's the first steps, a successful potty training, or a peaceful night of sleep. Recognize and appreciate the efforts of both parents, as this reinforces the bond between you and boosts morale. Creating a positive and supportive atmosphere will help you face future challenges with optimism and resilience.

In a nutshell, tag team parenthood is about building a strong partnership based on mutual support, communication, and shared responsibilities.

By working together as one, you can create a nurturing environment for your baby and strengthen your relationship as a couple. And you must bear in mind that your teamwork and commitment lay the foundation for a happy and fulfilling journey of parenthood, creating memories that will last a lifetime.

Part 2: The Second Trimester: Preparing for Parenthood

Chapter 5: Creating a Safe and Nurturing Environment

As an expecting parent, preparing a beautiful room for your little one will be one of the best feelings. Imagine how it will look, and how their curious eyes will wander around the room once they start understanding the things around them. At their tender age, they will have that kind of awesome feeling.

However, transforming your space for your little one might not be as easy as it seems. Don't get it twisted. What I'm saying is thinking about what you should put and what you shouldn't isn't an easy task, especially with all the excitement of awaiting their arrival.

In this chapter, I will discuss how you can create a safe and nurturing environment for your little one. I will also discuss how you can get them nesting chronicles alongside some Childproofing techniques so that even if this is the first time you are going to have a baby, you will be doing things as if you are a pro.

The Nesting Chronicles: Transforming Your Space for Tiny Tornadoes

Once the pregnancy enters the second trimester, you will want to start some preparations for your baby's arrival. This will be a nice idea because the earlier you do, the better. Because later, it might not be easy for you to do the up and downs. Even if you can hire someone for the work, as a first-time father, you will want to have the joy of doing it yourself. I will explain some of the steps and essentials you need to take note of when doing this joyful work.

Preparing the room
The first step is preparing the room you want for the baby. But before I reach there, I assume you have already chosen a baby room. If yes, I have this simple question, is it close to yours? If it's close, then that's bright. And if not, I suggest you should reconsider because the baby should be where you and her mother will easily hear her movements.

If the room is empty fine or if not, ensure you remove all the unnecessary items. Clean the room surface and the floor because babies are generally susceptible to allergies when exposed to dust, mold, and pet hair. Therefore, make sure you thoroughly clean the room and get rid of everything that can hinder your baby's health.

Also, when cleaning, use only a sponge and water, and mild chemical detergent. If the room has a bright light, consider changing it to a dimmer light. Oil your hinge doors, especially if they creak.

So whenever you get the baby to sleep, you can quietly shut the door without it making any sound.

Importantly, you should install safety features like smoke and carbon monoxide detector. If you wish, you can paint the nursery with a nontoxic paint that won't flake. So when they start to grow up; they can't peel the faint.

Furnish the room
If you already purchase the furniture, then check them and ensure that even if you arrange them outside, they can pass the door; if not, wait until the room is ready before you arrange them.

Also, put the crib according to the manufacturer's instructions. If you're not confident in your skills, look for a professional to set the crib for you. As a father, ensure to avoid using an old or modified crib. Make sure the mattress is firm, and ensure the space between the edges of the mattress and the side of the crib isn't more than two fingers width.

Put a comfortable chair in the room so you or the baby's mother can have where to sit down when you want to soothe him. You can also put a small mattress for you or the baby's mom because, in the first few months, one or two of you might be required to sleep there. In addition, you can use gilders and rockers, and you can also use oversized recliners and plush chairs.

Put on a dresser and changing table so you can organize the baby's clothes. You can also use a baby's closet or drawer, or cabinet. And remember to leave a space where you will keep the baby's diaper. Analyze the furniture and ensure they have met all safety standards.

Decorate the room

The theme you want to give the room entirely depends on your and your partner's preference. You can choose a simple color, and you can also get inspiration from a movie, or you can check online. If you still haven't found the one that suits your taste, then chevrons, the ocean, and birds are some of the common baby themes out there.

Decorate the wall according to the theme, even though they might not see it at an early stage. They will surely thank you once they reach the age of appreciating beauty. You can put fun things like framed pictures or even vintage toys. If you read illustrated storybooks, you can frame pages from there too. You can use Vinyl wall decals. They will give the room a unique visual impact without spoiling the wall.

Hung curtains that will blend with the room decor so you can give a cozy environment for your baby. Select a curtain that will block light. Because if they want to sleep in the afternoon they can still have a dim room. It's not recommended to use blinds in nurseries because their cord can harm children.

Only leave the crib with a mattress cover and sheet. Even if it tempts you to put toys inside the crib, avoid it and wait until the baby is at least one year old. You should also put two sheets in case the baby spits or has a diaper leak.

Hang a baby mobile if you wish to have one because the revolving baby monitor is used to soothe some babies. At the same time, some babies find it hard to sleep when it's on. Since you may not know whether your baby will like it, it's best to wait until they come before you purchase it.

Organizing baby's items
Avoid clutter in your baby's room. Aside from making it messy, too much clutter can be risky, especially when you want to enter the room in the dark. You can use different kinds of organizers to make the room look tidy such as cubbies, shelves, and containers. You can put them on top of the closet. Also, consider grouping similar items in the same place.

Arrange the diapers within arm's reach. This will make it easy for you when you want to change them because they are among the things you will use frequently. Get a diaper pail near the changing table so you can easily dispose of dirty diapers.

Set up a baby monitor and put the receiver where you used to be. This will keep your mind at ease, and whenever the baby starts crying or whimpering, you can respond quickly before they become upset. You can also purchase a visual baby monitor that enables you to view them when they are sleeping.

Well, fathers, too, wash their baby's clothes, so after you purchase them, consider washing them, especially if they aren't well packaged. Children's skin is extremely delicate, and some manufacturers coat new clothes with chemicals that will make them look grand and new in the shop. Moreover, different hands have likely touched the clothes. Therefore, it's best to wash them. Also, make sure the detergent you want to use is free from all chemicals, or it's specifically made for infants' use.

Find a space to store the baby's other essentials; as a first-time parent, you will be surprised to find how stuffy the baby's room will look after purchasing all the important items. Use the dresser, closet organizer, shelves, and any other available space to organize the baby's bibs, burp cloths, lotion, towels, toys, books, and other items. The things you will need to leave nearby are diapers, clothes hampers, a swing, and a bouncy seat.

Safety First, Laughs Later: Childproofing Like a Pro

Expecting a baby can bring a lot of new changes to your life. It's understandable to find yourself looking for the best ways to make your home a haven for your adorable one. Whether it's their nursery or the place you stay often, it's best to childproof everywhere in your home. The children are not going to remain in one stage. And since they are going to grow up and you don't know when they will decide to be mischievous, it's best to take all kinds of safety and precautionary measures as soon as possible.

Here are a few things you should do while childproofing like a pro:

Start from the bottom
The first place you should start when securing your home is the bottom. This is because your floor and ground are where your child will be frequently. That's where they will sit, crawl and walk too. Ensure every kind of object that is risky to them is removed and kept off the floor and totally out of their reach.

Additionally, vacuum and clean your floor regularly because harmful objects might not be visible to you, but they are still there and can harm your baby. You should never underestimate things when it comes to babies. This is because they can find something as small as deflated latex balloons or forgotten paper clips eatable, and they can be hazardous to them.

Once your baby grows up, constantly inspect their toys and play things.

Small pieces of toys may fall off, which can be harmful too. Immediately you notice a small piece from their toy on the floor, it's best to not only discard the piece but also throw away the toy.

You should frequently move your furniture to clear dirt. It might be surprising that those tiny humans can crawl, especially when playing, and reach under your furniture and find things that you have forgotten, like old batteries, buttons, loose papers, and many other related harmful things.

Secondly, secure all electric codes around the house. You can use zip ties, velcro, or cord straps to secure and remove cords from their reach. It's easy for your baby to become entangled with the wire or even pull them. You can secure the cords by wrapping the excess code length, then use a zip tie and secure it.

Use a command hook and hook the cord to the wall. Ensure to take the cord as high as possible. And when they become tall enough to reach it, by then, they know it's harmful to them. You can also use furniture to block sockets — this will block them from having access to the cord.

If you realize that rearranging your furniture isn't the best option, then here is another way you can childproof your home. Use plastic outlet covers around all the sockets. They will lie flat against the wall, making it hard for your baby to grab them. You can also use baby-safe electrical outlet plates over the existing outlets in your home. They will stick over the original outlet, and they look more appealing than plastic outlets.

Make a softer floor if your floor is hard. Once they reach a certain month, they will start to sit and crawl. And at this stage, they will need a soft surface so they won't injure themselves. There are a variety of soft carpets you can get from the market. You can also get baby play mats easily. So, you can lay one in their room and another in other areas accessible around the house.

Baby play mats come in different sizes and can be suitable for babies of different ages and sizes. If you want something else rather than the baby play mat let's say — a rug or carpet, then choose a dark shade piece. Both small and older babies are good at messing up intentionally or accidentally. So by choosing a dark shade rug, you can easily mask stubborn stains and leftover messes, and you won't feel the urge to change the rug.

Go up to windows and furniture
Once you are done with the ground, it's time to move up and baby-proof the upper aspect of your home.

The first place to start is the sharp edge of your furniture. You can use corner covers or bumpers to cover the place. Also, you can even get these items in local shops that sell children's things. It's easy to use, and you can remove them once the baby becomes older. The best aspect of these things is that some usually come in funny shapes like cartoons or animal-like characters. When buying, ensure to purchase enough to cover all the sharp edges of your home.
Secure bookcases and other tall furniture to the wall, especially when they age. Most babies love to grab anything they come across without caring about the dangers. Unfortunate things can happen like them grabbing an item, and it will fall on them.

If you purchase new furniture, you will enjoy some benefits because most new furniture these days comes with kits for securing the furniture to the wall. You can also get the kits at any nearby hardware store. All these items are easy to use and remove. So once you are done using them, you can remove them and rearrange your furniture.

Keep all your drawers closed and secure. You can use straps or locks to prevent the bundle of joy from accessing them. Think of the important things like small, fragile items, candles, and even sharp objects or lighters you usually keep inside the drawers. It will be hazardous if your child reaches them. Also, they will try to draw the drawers or use them as a ladder to climb up, which can lead to injury.

One of the best and easy ways to secure your drawer is to use installed magnetic locks. This key usually comes with multiple locks and one key. You can easily disable them if you want to open the drawers. And it won't allow your child to open even a crack. Because they can insert their finger if there is a crack, which can injure them.
Next is to secure your windows and window treatments. This will protect them because regardless of their height, they might want to grab the window latch. Therefore, you must ensure to secure your windows and the draperies and blinds. But babyproofing your windows depends on the type of window you have. For instance, if you have sliding windows, it's best to use a bar in the window track to prevent it from sliding open. If, on the other hand, you have the type of window that you will push out to open, then if they are closed, ensure the lock is properly put in to prevent them from opening again.

Secure all the cords hanging from your draperies and blinds because the cords can easily entangle your adorable one. You can use zip ties and command hooks to hold excess cords and hang them high so the child cannot get them.

If you have window glasses, make sure they are shatterproof. If not, then replace them before their arrival. Why I advise you to do all these in the second trimester is that you still have much time on your hand. Once the mother enters the third trimester, you won't find that much time to do them, and even if you do, it might not be as detailed as this. Put window guards to prevent them from falling

Secure doors and fixtures
The first door you should secure is the one in your living room because as they see people coming in and out, they might also want to try it, and in the process, they may end up going out or injuring themselves. You can use gadgets like door monkey or cover deadbolts to prevent them from unlocking the door. If you have a screen or storm door, use a metal mesh or grill on the bottom half to protect them from falling or pushing the screen out. Place a guard or barrier around fireplaces, space heaters, and radiators. Ensure your plants aren't poisonous, and place all breakable objects on high shelves.

We have come to the end of this chapter. Keep on reading for more amazing tips on how you can dad like a pro.

Chapter 6: Financial Planning for Parenthood

Nothing easily changes your life, like the arrival of a new human into your world. It comes with different emotions. One time, you will feel excited, and the other time you will feel nervous. I am sure you understand that raising a child isn't an easy task, and at times you will find yourself asking these simple yet important questions.

These questions could be: Do I have what it takes to raise this child? Do I need to make future financial preparations? The suitable answer is Yes. And the sweet part is that you get enough time to prepare since the baby is in its second trimester. You can do a lot of preparations before the baby's arrival.

In this chapter, I'm going to talk about financial planning for parenthood and some strategies you can follow so you can raise your baby comfortably.

Read on.

Diapers and Dollars: Managing Your Baby Budget with Style

It's hard to say, but diapers are getting expensive. And the worst part is that you will be spending dollars on something you will throw away, sometimes, a few minutes after putting it on the baby. I understand countless brands are cheap, but I believe you want to purchase something quality. Once you start using a quality diaper, it might be difficult to switch to other brands. But do you know there are many ways you can save and budget for diapers without going broke along the line?

Here are some ways you can manage your baby's budget with style:

- Use coupons

This is one of the best ways I advise expecting parents to manage their budget styles regarding baby products. You will always find coupons for at least $1 off Huggies, Pampers, and other children's items. Once you combine that with the sales price, you will be surprised at how much you have saved. You can get a pack of diapers for $5 or less. Also, you can get a pack of wipes with little money too.

- Be slow when changing sizes

Why do I mention this? Because if you observe, the bigger the diaper size, the fewer they will be inside the package and the more expensive it will be. All diapers come with sizes in the pack, but what I understand from my years of experience is that children can wear a diaper size longer than what the brand suggests. For example, your baby can weigh less than what the diaper brand made for children of their age. And the ones you usually use for them, which aren't meant for them. You can still fit them without any leak, which means instead of changing it to what it's created for their age, you can easily stick to the one you've been using. Furthermore, you should consider changing the size once you understand there are leaks or the size is small for them.

- Be mindful of the way you put a diaper

Once your baby arrives, there are small tricks you can use to stick to using a diaper longer than expected. The first thing you should observe is how your baby's leak usually comes out. If it's from behind, then while putting the diaper on them, pull it up more in the back. And if it's from the front, then pull it up more in the front.

If you try all these tricks and none work, then I have no other way to solve your problem. Therefore, you have to change the diaper size.

- Watch package size

Rather than thinking about the price of each pack, think of the price of each diaper inside the pack. Confusing right? Let me clear up this confusion. It's not all packages that contain the same amount of product. For example, you will find a product with more pieces inside and the only difference is in the brand's name.

Pampers Soft Care wipes come in 72-count packages, while Pampers Sensitive wipes come in 64-count packages. These products go for the same price, but if you want the 64 counts, you should go for one that has a high number.

You can also find things like this in diapers: Huggies Snug & Dry Size 2 comes in 42-count packages, while Huggies Little Snugglers size two only has 36 per package. And they all go for the same price. But if you choose the one with 42 counts, you will see that you have saved $0.04 on each diaper.

- Stockpile

What most parents fail to understand is that stockpiling is highly important. You may want to buy things when you need them the most, but believe me, stockpiling is a joyful way of saving. And you might not understand that until you see how much you have saved.

Any product you find at a low price may be during a bonanza, then ensure to buy even if you won't need to use them immediately. You will save small compared to buying them when you need them. Also, you should take baby stockpiling seriously whenever you see any item at rock bottom price.

Since the pregnancy is in the second trimester, you still have at least 4-5 months before the due date. So from now, if you start buying, you may purchase what will last you a year or even more.

- Try new brands

If you want to maximize your savings and stick to your budget. Then, you must be willing to try other brands once in a while. The idea is that sometimes you will see that some brands are cheaper than others. But one way to be safe when using a new brand is to ask around.

You can join different children's care groups where you will find similar people like you that interact with each other. If you find any cheap brand, you can ask people from the group, or you can go to the product website and check for people's reviews. Once you find one worth the price, you can buy it.

As a recommendation, you can purchase Costco and Target brand diapers. Based on the review I obtained, they are decent and go at an affordable price. Furthermore, remember that in most of the stores for baby products, you will find a money-back guarantee. So if you find one that has issues, you can return it and get your money which means you won't lose even a dime.

- Buy in bulk

Another best way to stay on budget is to buy everything in bulk. Most baby brands come with a bonus when you want to buy plenty. For example, you can find a unique brand that is willing to give you some percentage off if you want to buy a certain amount of their product.

You can also find one that can deliver it for free if you can buy their product's specific amount. Whichever you get, it's an opportunity you shouldn't let slip.

Insurance, Investing, and Inevitable Expenses: Navigating the Money Maze

Getting your finance ready is one of the important ways you can prepare for the baby's arrival. While you may focus your attention on the medical activities related to your baby, I assure you that dividing your attention and leaving some for how you can navigate through the financial stages is also important. Also, the sooner you start planning for your baby's arrival, the better. Here I will explain how you can navigate the money maze once you see those two lines in the pregnancy test. Why I said from the early stage of pregnancy is because you don't need to wait for the second or third trimester to start financial planning; starting early is always the best.

Here is how you can go about it:

- First month

In the first month of pregnancy, you should reduce your credit card debt. You should transfer your money to a credit card that has lower interest. Because if you calculate the interest expenses you spend at the end of the year, you will see that it's something big. Still, in the first month of pregnancy, you should keep track of your spending. Unless you earn more than your usual money. Then, it's best to create a new budget. Keep track of your big and small expenses to understand your spending habits better. You should keep a receipt or find a book where you will write down whatever you buy. When the time comes when you will reduce these expenses, that's in the third month. This tracking will help you determine how you spend the money and the areas you need to cut down.

- Second month

In the second month, you will still be keeping a record of your expenses, continuing your life as you used to, and ensuring you maintain current beneficiaries. After some time in the second month, update your beneficiaries, and delete any outdated beneficiaries on your company-sponsored life insurance and a 401k plan, especially if you started your job without marriage. Once you evaluate your beneficiaries, you may likely find people you no longer need to credit their account, for example, your ex-girlfriend, sister, or even parents sometimes.

- The third month

In the third month, you should analyze your credit rating. Use the information you have been recording and create a more detailed budget. Sometimes, although you pay your bills on time always, there might be a time when you make some errors, sit down and correct all those mistakes. As a parent-to-be, it's important to have a strong and good credit record, and maybe you are planning to purchase a house or car. As time goes on in the third month, it's time to crunch the numbers, which will be your last step in making a budget. Take the numbers from all the expenses and write them in another sheet or insert them in a budget tracking app. You will get a clear picture of your spending, then start doing a makeover on the list in preparation for the big day your baby will arrive. The goal is to save something so you will invest it later. Now it's time to create a new budget. When doing that, always put your baby in mind — you will feel like your income is now smaller, but I assure you with a good budget, you will do everything accordingly without experiencing any hardship.

- The fourth month

The fourth month is the best time to assess the experience your baby will take out of your income. This could be before and after they are born and how much time they will also take from your work, especially if you are a business person. Also, the first step during this month is to make a paternity friend in HR. Get the full benefit from your human resources department.

Federal law requires you to give at least 30 days' notice when requesting time off under the Family and Medical Leave Act. This is because any new parent who works for a company with at least 50 employees can take up to 12 weeks of unpaid, seniority-protected leave. Your employer must provide the usual healthcare benefits during this time.

The next thing to do is to practice austerity. You set a new budget last month, and now that the baby is yet to come, you will feel like keeping the new budget aside and waiting until the baby arrives before you start using it. It would help if you never did that. That could be among the biggest mistakes you will make in this period.

This is the second trimester, so you should eliminate all unnecessary things. It's best to furnish the nursery now — so, start planning. You should set aside financial goals for that.

- Fifth month

By the time you reach the fifth month, you have reached the midpoint of the pregnancy journey. And this is the best time to start considering the childcare products you want for the baby.

- Sixth month

The sixth month is a great time to nitty items like life insurance and will. As an expectant parent, I would recommend getting yourself insured at least six times or even eight times your annual income to cover anticipated dependents. Cash-value policies like whole life, variable life, and universal life are complicated and sometimes a bad move, especially since you can make interest from other means like tax-deferred and tax-free investments like retirement accounts and college savings plans. The next thing to do is to write a will, regardless of how you want to live.

Nobody knows what will happen tomorrow. You may loathe to decide the best person to raise your child in case you or their mother leave. Due to this, you can write a Will to decide who will be your baby's guardian if you pass on before they are born. You can hire a lawyer when you are ready to draft a will, and you should expect to spend around $500 to $1000.

- Seventh month

In the seventh month, you should consider saving for your baby's college funds. You can join a college savings program like the Upromise, which can help you save for your baby's future even before you name them.

- Eighth month

Your parents might already be planning for your big day and the kind of gift they will give you. And you will be surprised how generous people are to upcoming parents. People give a lot of gifts, sometimes you might even receive some basic baby needs. You can open a saving box where you will save some of the gifts. Some people may give you monetary items, put in mind these funds are not yours; it's for your adorable ones. So find a separate account, and you will save it for them. Still, in the eighth month, keep your eyes on retirement. Even though you may think this isn't the best time for this, you should always put it among the goals you want to prioritize.

- Ninth month and beyond

As the baby is nearing the due date, it's essential to stick to your new budget and save as much money as possible. It's also time to take the step of getting an insurance baby for your new family member. Most health insurance companies allow new parents to add their newborn baby to their policy thirty days after delivery. You can check with your human resources and carrier. You can also start filling out the enrollment form. After that, you can leave the baby's birth date and name blank if you still haven't decided on a name for them. Since you might be busy when the baby arrives, you should think of the person you will assign to fill in the blanks once the baby arrives and submit the form to HR.

Chapter 7: The Journey to Labor and Delivery: The Second Trimester

The second trimester usually lasts from week 14 to week 27. And for most people, this is the best part of their pregnancy journey. It is the best, especially for expectant mothers, because they have passed the stage of fatigue and morning sickness, which usually happen in the first trimester. At this stage, the baby has developed (has added weight) and has already started assuming a human form. Still, at this phase, your pregnant partner should have an ultrasound. That is if you wish to know the baby's gender and to ensure the baby is growing perfectly.

By the end of the second trimester, the baby will start moving. However, you have to bear in mind that the pregnancy journey is different for everyone. What happened to your partner might be different from what happened to other expectant mothers. You might be surprised to know that some people never experienced all these pregnancy symptoms. They had a smooth ride from beginning to end while others will experience a roller coaster to the extent they will feel like giving up. But everything I have been describing in this book is taken from the majority.

Now, it's time to go into the details of the labor and delivery journey. Don't shiver; you have to man up and be strong for your partner and baby.

Cravings, Contractions, and Craziness: Supporting Your Partner through the Adventure

As a concerned father, you must comfort your pregnant partner from the start to the end of the journey. I know there is a little you can do to help your partner bear the pain of pregnancy or labor. But do you know there are many other ways you can be fully involved in this journey? And these acts can go a long way to help ease her discomfort and take her mind off the pregnancy. Check out some of the ways:

- Talk to her

The first step in helping your partner is to provide her with listening ears and a shoulder to lean on. I understand it might be overwhelming for both of you at the beginning. But talking to each other, and expressing your feelings can make both of you feel better. So, keep your communication line widely open because it will help you.

- Cheer and comfort her

The second thing to remember is that she will be moody sometimes. These usually happen due to hormonal changes, exhaustion, tiredness, and discomfort in general. She might be laughing one time and start crying within a few minutes. You should understand her at this stage. Offer her a shoulder to cry, comfort her, and tell her everything is well. Even if she snaps at you, be patient. The entire period will only last for nine months.

- Accept her cravings

She might enjoy a certain food today and throw up tomorrow at the mere smell of it. Also, she might crave something you will find ridiculous. In this situation, try to understand her. Those are not her doings — it is because of the hormonal changes she is experiencing. Support every choice she makes regarding food except the ones that may harm the baby.

- Accompany her during doctor visits

Although you have your schedules, if you can, make time and accompany her for the hospital visits. This will mean a lot to her. Hold her hand during the ultrasound. If you do that once, you wouldn't want to stop because there is nothing better than seeing the tiny human through the ultrasound machine and hearing their heartbeat. You will be thrilled to see the memories you will make during this time.

- Educate yourself about pregnancy

Well, I can tell that's the very reason you are reading this book. Although the book contains everything you are looking for regarding pregnancy and how you will help your wife, you can still incorporate it with other books about the pregnancy journey for fathers.

- Make sure she receives adequate nutrition

While she may want to stick to her cravings, you should ensure she eats healthily. Your home should never lack healthy foods like fruit and proteins. You can also healthily make her cravings. For example, if she craves something unhealthy, you can match it with healthy food. This way, she will feel satisfied, and at the same time, you are also helping her.

I will keep repeating this, even if she gets angry at you; understand that it's not her doings. She doesn't want that as well, but her hormones can make her do all sorts of things.

- Allow her to rest and get some sleep

Do you know your partner's body does much work even if she sleeps? This means she will need time to sleep and rest more than she used to before the pregnancy. Increase the percentage of housework you usually do, and take some from her so she can sleep more. This doesn't mean you shouldn't allow her to do any work. The house chores are beneficial for her health, and they will help her during labor. Always give affectionate hugs and kisses — they are a great encouragement.

- Don't reduce your intimacy

Intimacy here might not necessarily mean sex. Just be more affectionate — hug, kiss, cuddle, and caress her more during this time. In the first trimester, it might not be convenient for her to have sex with you. She can easily get tired and overwhelmed, but regardless of the situation, never stop cuddling her. Those romantic touches are still important to her — they make her feel loved. The attention you give her will make her feel secure even if she isn't feeling great about her body.

- Help her with exercise

Your Partner needs to perform some mild exercises which will ease her labor. You can seek help from her doctor on the kind of exercise she can engage in. If she isn't motivated to exercise, you can go out to exercise and then ask her to accompany you. A simple walk together can go a long way to help her.

- The answer whenever she calls

Sometimes she might call you for a silly reason, and it might be an emergency. Whatever the situation is, always answer her calls.

The Birth Plan Chronicles: Making Joint Decisions and Surviving the Delivery Room Drama

Parents usually make birth plans so they will know what to expect during their delivery. As the father, you want to be involved in every aspect of the pregnancy. There is no specific time when you will start making birth plans.

Your partner may already have an idea of the kind of labor she wants. So when drafting the birth plan, help her write what's only necessary to her because writing plenty of information will confuse you and the other caregivers. There are also many apps specifically created for making a birth plan. You can use one and ensure that aside from you, another person has a copy of the birth plan. What you should include in the birth plan should be her preference, and what she would love to avoid.

Some things you should decide regarding the birth plan include the following:

- What are her wishes during delivery and labor

This can be how she hopes to handle the pain, the fetal monitoring, etc. You should talk about the environment she wants to have the baby in, does she want someone else aside from you to be with her? And what kind of birth position she wants to employ?

- How does she hope for the baby to be treated after birth

Does she want you to cut the baby cord, or do you wish to do it?

Would she want the baby on her stomach immediately after birth, or would she want to feed the baby first? Is it breastfeeding or bottle feeding? Would she want the baby to be placed close to her while they slept, or would want them to be put inside a nursery?

Most hospitals have different ways of caring for a baby after birth. So before you write this part, you should visit (together or alone) the hospital you wish for her to give birth to and speak with them to see if their rules align with what the two of you want.

- What does she want in case of unforeseen circumstances?

Although nobody wants something bad to happen, especially on this big day. There might be inevitable things, so it's best to plan and have some options in advance. Some women may require cesarean section during their childbirth. Therefore, you should discuss with her if the labor takes unexpected turns. This is what may happen. You should also talk about other situations like premature birth and decide what will happen in that case.

Note

Before you start making any decisions regarding any of these birth plan options, you should talk to your healthcare provider first. Perhaps, the hospital already has a birth plan form where you will sit with your partner, go through it and fill out the form. You can use the form as a guideline to prepare yours. You can also look for a hospital that matches your birth plans so everything will be easy for the two of you. It's also necessary to be flexible. For example, if there is something on your list that isn't on their list, you can weigh it and see if there is a way you can compromise.

Also, talk to the hospital if something about the pregnancy might prevent some of your choices. The hospital might also prevent you from following some of your birth plans.

So now it's time to think of where you want or if she wants to have her baby. While many women usually give birth in the hospital. Today, women are no longer confined in the sterile maternity ward when giving birth. Some hospitals practice family-centered care where a patient's room will feature a bathroom, furniture, and adequate space to accommodate family members.

Also, some hospitals provide birthing rooms that enable pregnant women to be in the same bed for labor, delivery, and postpartum care. They usually equipped the room fully with all necessities in case of a complicated delivery. Immediately you see the room, it will attract your attention with its furnishings and gentle lighting.

Some women find comfort in their homes rather than hospitals; these women believe that childbirth should happen at home. In this case, you should talk to your partner about their preference regarding where they want to give birth. If they feel like giving birth at home will be their choice, then you can discuss all the safety measures that will ensure safe delivery.

- Who will assist during the childbirth

Women usually choose an obstetrician that will help them during the child's delivery. This is a person specifically trained to handle all kinds of pregnancies. So if the pregnancy is considered complicated, your partner will be referred to a skilled medical practitioner. In your childbirth plan, you can also choose to have a family practitioner who is trained in managing non-risk pregnancies. The advantage of working with a family doctor is that, even after delivery, they will continue to take care of your partner and the baby.

The Labor Diaries: What to Expect When Your Partner Is Expecting

This is your first time being a dad, so it's understandable that you don't know many things about childbirth. Know that there are a few things you should keep in mind once your partner is in labor. I will explain what you should expect and the planning you should do even before the labor phase kickstarts.

Below are the details you should pay keen attention to:

- Plan the hospital route

The first step to preparing for labor is which route to follow to the hospital. It would help to consider the traffic that usually happens at different times on the road. Know that if the journey happens during rush hour or school times, then it will take longer time to reach the hospital. If you plan to hire a taxi, then before the due date, contact a different taxi company and make plans with them.

- Is she in labor?

Once she enters the third trimester and is approaching her EDD, she may likely experience contractions. But these contractions are different from normal contractions; she won't feel pain, and they don't build up. They are just uncomfortable. The actual sign of labor includes water breakage (a gushing of fluid).

Once she starts experiencing this practice of contractions, labor will follow 12 hours after. Maybe you are used to movies where the water breaks before contraction. In real life, contractions usually start before water breakage. Other signs of true labor include persistent back pain and cramp that feels like premenstrual feeling.

- Time her contractions

Normally, contractions happen at intervals, and as time goes on, they used to get longer and stronger. You should time her contraction from the beginning of one to the start of the next one. Her physician has likely left a number to contact. So once the contractions start coming every five minutes and last for about 45 to 60 seconds, you should contact the physician's number. They will advise you on the best time to go to the hospital.

- Timing is important

Once they find that your partner is in her early labor stage, they will do an antenatal assessment on her. If nothing is found, they ask you to return home until the labor fully begins. So while she's experiencing the contractions and it's not yet time to go to the hospital, you should try your best to take her mind off it. You can watch movies, give her a hot bath, get her something healthy to eat, or help her rest for some time.

The idea behind this is that a study has shown that women rest more when in their comfortable environment, such as their home, than when they are in the hospital. It will also be tiring and discomforting to be in the hospital when it's not the due time — she will feel like time is not moving.

- Know what's coming

Sometimes, as in the movie, a baby can be born so quickly, but this usually happens on rare occasions. For most women, especially first-timers, labor can last 12 to 16 hours. Generally, early labor that usually happens at home can take hours or days sometimes.

Once she enters the first stage of labor, you should expect it to last for five to six hours, and at this stage, you should get her to the hospital. You will see her huffing and puffing, and I assure you be prepared to experience some mixed emotions.

Get ready for some unusual attitude from them, too, because, in this stage, they can do anything. She can even blame everything on you, so getting ready for this ranting and putting it in mind is pretty normal. You should know that you will always be there with her, help her, ask her to inhale and exhale, and rub her back and feet too. Prepare a drink nearby, so whenever she needs it, you will give her. In this stage, do whatever she asks you to do as long as it is within your means.

- The baby's arrival

It's time for the baby's arrival now; although you will feel overwhelmed, you should also consider what you will do. Do you wish to film this emotional moment to keep it for history? Once the baby is out, what will follow is the placenta, which can take up to five to sixty minutes to follow. She may feel cold at this time or even shaky. So your eyes should remain on her and prepare a blanket in case she needs some warmth.

- After the birth

Depending on when your partner gives birth, she may not be allowed to eat until after several hours. You might find it difficult to predict what she would love to eat after giving birth because even if you include this in the birth plans, they might be changed, and she will feel like eating another thing. So prepare a few options she can choose from. For the remaining time, she will be in the hospital, and after the first few days she returns home, trying as much as possible to refrain from doing any work. Help her with the baby and other housework; she might want to be alone, but ensure you are close to her all the time, satisfying her needs.

And that's all for the second part of this book.

Part 3: The Third Trimester: Mastering Newborn Care

Chapter 8: The First Days with Your Newborn

No baby ever comes with a manual on handling him from the womb. Rather babies tend to turn your life upside down to the extent that you will begin to wonder: Will my life ever be the same again? Things will certainly change, but you must establish new routines immediately after they arrive. Luckily, you have this amazing book as a guide, and I can assure you that it will make a tremendous difference, which you can attest to.

In this chapter, I will explain what it looks like after having your baby, their appearance and behavior after some time, and even a survival guide to navigate this phase. Get ready to catch some amazing tips in the following sections:

From Delivery Room to Dadeville: Welcoming Your Little Rockstar with Open Arms

In the early days, after birth, the mother would take care of everything regarding the baby. Often, fathers feel left out, and sometimes, they are the ones that don't want to get involved with their babies. Well, things have already changed for the good now. You will see nearly 90% of new fathers having a strong bond with their newborn babies right from the delivery room. So now, as a new father in this system, how can you welcome your little one with an open arm?

Below are what you should prioritize and pay attention to:

- Start with an early interaction

Dr. John Klaus and Phyllis Klaus, in their book, "Your Amazing Newborn," said that the first way to create a bond with your new baby as their father is to connect with them as early as possible. That means a few minutes or hours after their birth. If you can, play with them even if they don't understand what you are doing, and ensure to have eye-to-eye contact constantly, especially in the first three months. Babies tend to sleep most of the time, and if they aren't sleeping, they will probably be with their mothers eating. So, you can seize the opportunity when she wants to bathe or enter the restroom and bond with your baby.

- Have skin-to-skin contact with them

Aside from bonding with your baby, skin-to-skin contact offers many other benefits like temperature regulation, reduce stress, stabilize blood sugar, and oxytocin release (if you aren't familiar with oxytocin hormone, then know that it's a love hormone, it's usually released when a person is in a happy mood.) It will also give you comfort and security. You should have skin-to-skin contact with your baby when you are opportune. In the delivery room, once everything is settled and the baby is being fed, you can find a comfortable chair and sit down, remove your shirt, and ask the nurse or midwife to place the baby on your chest. They should cover the two of you with a blanket and let you enjoy the wonderful moment. To be honest, there is nothing sweeter than the smell and touch of a new baby.

- Sing to your baby

This should begin when they are still in the womb. Many doctors believe that singing to your baby the same song you usually sing for them when they are in the uterus can be a great way to bond with them. You don't have to wait for them to start crying before you sing for them. Rather, you can sing for your baby while you are having a good time holding them and making eye contact; they will recognize your voice whenever they hear it.

- Bath with them

Most new babies love to bathe together with their parents. They like that feeling when they are cradled in your arms. Although new babies don't need frequent bathing, still, whenever you get the chance, take a bath with them in a moderate water temperature while they relax on your chest. While the baby feels secure and comfortable, you will feel relaxed. But for safety purposes, have the mother stand close by holding the baby while you enter the hub, and when you finish, you will give them the baby before you exit the tub.

- Read to your baby

Even though they might not understand what you are saying at the early stage, you should still read for them. Generally, newborn babies are fascinated with human language and how to talk. Once they reach two to three months, you will observe that they will look at your mouth whenever you talk. If you read a newspaper, magazine, or novel, you should be reading it out loud so your baby will also hear; as they age, you can start reading books appropriate for their age.

- Baby wear them

Most children love it when their parents' baby wears them. This is also another great chance for you to establish a solid connection. You can safely wear them in your free time or even create a time out of your hectic schedule. Also, if you are going out or want to do some tasks, you can easily wear your baby and walk around with them. You can find different carriers in the market. So, during your shopping, you should buy one that will be convenient for you and the baby.

- Exercise

Once your baby reaches the mouth when they can be safely exposed to the outside, you should take them out when you are going for an exercise. You can get a baby carrier or stroller for this. As they age, you can safely put them on your bike seat or use a bike trailer. You should always follow the instructions with the carrier to be on the safe side.

Alien or Adorable? Decoding Newborn Appearance and Behaviors

After your baby is born, your physician might assure you everything is normal about him, but at the same time, you may find that your baby looks slightly different compared to how you see babies. In this situation, don't panic. Newborn babies can have peculiar characteristics, but these things are temporary. Once they reach one or two weeks, they will start to look normal. What I will explain regarding children's appearance will be arranged based on body parts.

- Head

Perhaps your baby's head looks long, narrow cone-shaped; this is because they pass through a tight birth canal. So the head will compress and temporarily hide the fontanel, rest assured, the head will return to normal after a few days.

Your baby can also swell on top of their head or in the entire scalp; this is not something to panic about; this usually happens when water is squeezed into the scalp during childbirth, and it will clear within a short time.

It's also possible for blood to collect on the outer part of the skull. This condition is called Cephalohematoma. It's because of friction between the baby's head and the mother's pelvis. If you notice a lump on one side of their head, it will go on once they reach two to three months.

You will also find a soft spot on top of your head; this is usually common and happens in every newborn. The soft spot is to enable the brain to grow rapidly, so as they get older, you will notice the spot filling by itself, and it will become solid.

- Eyes

You may observe swollen eyes on your baby. This is due to pressure put on the face during delivery. The eyes can also be irritated, but it will go after three days.

Flamed-shaped bleeding can also happen, which is natural and due to birth trauma. It will usually leave after three weeks. Their iris can also have different colors, including blue, green, gray, or brown, or variations of these colors. They won't have a permanent iris color until they reach six months. Their eyes can also be continuously watery because of blocked tear ducts. The blocked duct will open once they reach twelve months.

- Ears

One of the ears can fold at the early stage of birth. It will go back to normal once the cartilage hardens.

- Nose

The nose can be misshapen because of the birth process. It will return to normal after one week.

- Mouth

You may observe a sucking callus at the center of their upper lip or their thumb or wrist. For the lip, because of the friction of not being used to breastfeeding, it will leave once they grasp how to feed properly.

Newborn behavior
Although babies usually develop at different rates and phases, they still have some common behaviors. Note that babies that are born prematurely are different from full-term babies. These babies usually develop at a slower rate. Still, if you observe them develop phenomenally, even though they are born premature, you should immediately contact your healthcare provider. Some of the normal behaviors of newborn babies include

- Sleeping

Babies can sleep for up to 20 hours a day. The remaining 4 hours will usually be used for feeding because they have a small stomach which can't keep them full for a long time.

- Crying

The best way babies convey a message to us, adults, is through crying. But there are times they will cry for no reason. Once they start crying, it's their way of telling you they want something. Usually, new babies cry when they are hungry, tired, cold, or hot, want you to change their diaper, are over-stimulated, or when are sick. They can also commonly hiccup, sneeze, yawn, spit, burn, and gurgle. If they are crying and it is not due to any of these underlying reasons, you should try to comfort them by rocking them, backing them, singing for them, or wrapping them comfortably. If you try and still fail, don't panic; these adorable creatures don't know what they are doing. Ask their mother or someone else to help you handle them. Also, avoid shaking your baby; it can lead to brain damage and lifelong disability.

- Reflexes

Normally, during the first few days after birth, children tend to maintain their position in the womb.

Their fist is clenched, elbows bent, and their arms are closed to their body. This is because they don't have control over their movement once they can assume the normal position. They also have plenty of reflexes.

For example, they turn in the direction of food; this is called rooting reflexes. They also immediately start sucking once you place nipples inside their mouth; it's known as the sucking reflex. They also show startle reflexes accompanied by crying by throwing their arms and legs and then curling them. Tonic reflexes happen when they turn their head to a side and hold their arm on the same side. The grasp reflex happens when they hold a thing with their fingers strongly (if you have a beard, get ready to experience this, those creatures are very strong when it comes to this, I'm a living witness.) They can also imitate stepping when you hold them standing with their feet on your body or the floor. Their arms and cheeks can also tremble when crying because their nervous system is partially developed at this stage.

- Breathing

It's also common for new babies to have irregular breathing patterns. They can stop breathing for about five to ten seconds and then instantly continue breathing. When this happens, don't worry, it's common. However, if you observe they aren't breathing for more than ten seconds, instantly contact your doctor or take them to a nearby emergency room.

- Vision

Newborns are born with good eyesight, but you may observe their eyes looking crossed. This is because they can't focus. For the first few months, they see movement and the differences between black and white objects. Once they reach two to three months, they will start to have control over their eye muscles, enabling them to focus on a thing once in a while.

- Hearing

Newborns can perfectly hear and can differentiate between sounds and voices. This is another opportunity for you to always talk to your bundle of joy so they can recognize your voice even on call. The sound of human speech at first might seem like music to them with a different tone and rhythm.

Hospital Hijinks: A Dad's Survival Guide to Navigating the Baby Bubble

In the first few months after your baby's arrival, it's hard to get used to it. This is understandable, but the best thing you should do is to establish a routine. However, you can't just impose a routine on your baby and expect it to start working. Rather, you will slowly work with their routine while trying to make it favorable to you. You can decide when to make them sleep by singing or reading.

Another way to survive your baby's bubble, which you have probably seen the nurse in the hospital doing, is by swaddling them like a burrito. The swaddling act comforts them; it makes them feel like they are still in the womb. You don't even need to purchase a new swaddle. You can use the one you got from the hospital.

Additionally, sleeping is important for you and the baby. It plays a major role in your ability to focus and be productive entirely. You can take the popular advice of sleeping when the baby sleeps or staying awake when the baby is awake, but you should always try and maintain a healthy resting schedule. Stick to a good bedtime, watch your caffeine intake, and once you feel tired, sit and relax. It would help if you also take care of yourself in general.

While you may need to change some lifestyle, that doesn't mean you should stop doing what you are used to. Don't allow your schedule to dominate your life, and also don't allow taking care of your baby to make you forget your priorities. You can continue doing healthy activities like exercise; do your hobbies and everything you enjoy. Ensure to do other house chores, too. As I have said earlier, you can always back the baby while busy.
Furthermore, remember that you mustn't do this alone. While the baby has you and your partner, you may still need to include other family members; this way, you will build a support network that will motivate you and help you feel confident. You can as well join a parenting group where many fathers chat and exchange some information regarding parenthood. As a first-time father, this will help you a lot.

If you encounter a problem that is beyond what you know and you don't feel like talking to your partner or family, you can always seek help from your buddies in the parenting group. Generally, you should always remember that patience and self-regulation are key. It's among the valuable things you can cultivate as a parent, and you should learn it from your firstborn so you will find it easy subsequently. You will start dealing with a small human that doesn't know anything about the world. Before you know it, they will grow up and become big that you will feel joy whenever you look at them.

Chapter 9: Diaper Duty and Baby Basics

In this life, there are many things that we can do within a short time. These may look easy, but until you are asked or you need to do it, that's when you will know that such work is filled with hardship. But with little practice, you will become a pro in doing this work. In this chapter, I will discuss diaper duty and other baby basics. I will describe some hilarious hazards related to diapers, feeding frenzy, and how you can groom your adorable baby with Finesse.

Diaper Disasters and Hilarious Hazards: Conquering the Art of Diaper Changing

By now, I know that you must be longing to see your baby. The thought of that is even cherishable and invaluable. However, are you getting yourself prepared for some of the duties that await you? Let me be specific, do you know you have to equip yourself with the skill of diaper changing? Oh! Nobody has told you about that. Now, you have it for free.

The thought of changing a diaper as a father might be terrifying, but guess what? I have good news. I will share with you a few tips on how to change your baby's diaper.

- Start by cleaning the changing area

You should constantly clean your baby's bum to disinfect the place. This will prevent them from rashes and infection too. If you use a diaper changing pad, you should always change that on time. Aside from these things, everything you use while changing the diaper should also get washed, especially if it gets dirty. What you should be after is the safety of your baby. You should ensure that they are cleaned thoroughly so they will remain healthy.

- Stock up

The second thing you should take care of is that when it's time for you to change diapers, everything is close by. You can arrange the wipes, the new diaper, water if necessary, and the dustbin you want to discard the used diaper close to you. This will help you be with them, and you will do the work quickly.

- Find a perfect place to change

This can be their nursery or any safe place in your home. You should stick to it, and it should be far from other important areas in your home, like the kitchen or dining area. Your changing place will be a place that may attract germs since you will be dealing with dirt there, so constantly clean it all the time.

- Find some distractions

When you place your baby in the changing area, they may feel restless and want to wiggle around, especially if they have grown up. So find something that will distract them because if they aren't staying still, they may hurt themselves or even splash dirt on you. Get them a toy to play with or play some music for them, or even sing so it will take their mind off the work, and you will finish quickly and easily.

- Keep a separate diaper bin

It would help if you can separate your diaper bin from the one you put other dirt. You can also use nylon inside the bin so it won't directly taint it. Once it is piled up, you can take the nylon and fold it, then dispose of it.

- Use the best wipes

Finding the best wipes is highly important. It will help clean your baby thoroughly, and you should also find one that is safe for their skin. You know how delicate your baby's skin is, right? So, you should be careful with the product you will use on them. Also, clean their hands and feet to remain on the safe side.

- Wash their hands

After wiping their hands with the wipes, use water and wash their hands and feet.

How to change a diaper

Before changing your baby's diaper, you need to have some necessities close by.
- Change of clothes for your baby
- Changing table
- Diaper
- Diaper cream
- Dustbin
- Wipes

The steps I'm going to explain are for changing disposable diapers.

- Get ready: Wash your hands first and then prepare your supplies.
- Remove the dirty diaper: Lay your baby gently on the changing area and unfasten the diaper's pad from each side. Hold their ankle and gently lift their bottom from the diaper and then remove the diaper. If the diaper is really spoiled, then use the upper half and sweep it toward the lower half. Remove the diaper and then put it inside the disposable bin.
- Clean the baby's bottom: Once you discard the diaper, your baby's bottom will have dirt remnants, so wipe and clean them. If your baby is a girl, use the wipe and clean their vulva from front to back to prevent infection. If it's a boy, clean all the areas around the penis and scrotum. To avoid hilarious diaper disasters, put a clean wipe on their private part so they won't pee on your face while you are cleaning them.
- Put on a clean diaper: Once you finish cleaning them, get your clean diaper. Hold their ankle and lift their bottom, then gently slide it and let them lay down on the diaper. Keep the tabs on the side.

You will know the front and back of the diaper; the one with tabs is back, and they won't be fit to wear without the tab in the front. Place your baby's penis downward to prevent them from peeing outside. Use diaper ointment for rash and infection prevention. Pull the diaper front between the legs and allow it to reach the lower belly. Open the tabs at the side and gently put them around the front. Ensure not to tighten it, and don't make it too loose.

You may be asking how long you should change your baby's diaper. To be sincere, this entirely depends on how often your baby spoils it. You should change it as soon as it gets spoiled. As a newborn baby, you should expect them to use at least ten or more diapers a day, and as they grow up, the number will reduce. Urine and stool can irritate their skin, so avoid leaving them with it for a long time.

Feeding Frenzy: Breast, Bottle, and the Great Solids Showdown

Initially, you won't be much help feeding because they will only feed on your partner's breast. But, as time passes, you must use the bottle to feed them. This bottle can be used to give them water and also breast. Here are some tips for feeding.

- Your baby should be comfortable

The first step in feeding your baby is to sit in a comfortable space. You might be tempted to sit on the couch in front of your TV, but the light might blind your baby. Also, you may be tempted to sit and feed while watching your favorite Netflix video, but you must focus on the task too. In essence, you have to refrain from doing that. And if you must use your phone while doing the job, you should reduce the brightness or turn the light to night mode so it won't bother your baby.

- Hold the baby upright at the beginning of the feeding

It's best to hold them upright at the beginning of the feeding, especially if the bottle is full. This will enable them to control the flow. Support your baby's head and back so they can be firmly secured in your arms and make them comfortable.

- Hold the bottle horizontally at the beginning of the feeding

At the beginning of the feeding, when the bottle is full, hold it horizontally. There will be no drips. It can make them choke when the milk is poured too much, so this position will ensure a steady flow.

- Hold the bottle steadily

When your baby is feeding directly from their mom's breast, she will hold them steadily so they can remain latching on the breast, and they can even pause while feeding. That's safe with the breast, but different with bottles. When feeding them with a bottle, you don't only need to hold the baby steadily, but you must also hold the bottle properly too. You can get them a bottle that also works like a breast so they can feed and pause at their will without encountering any problems.

- Watch out and ensure the nipple tip always have milk

Always watch and ensure that the teat is filled with milk, and amazingly you will see how your adorable one is looking into your eyes. As I mentioned earlier, having eye contact with your baby is highly important because it will create a strong bond between you. Also, by knowing that the teat is filled with milk, you will rest assured that they are drinking, not just inhaling air. As the milk keeps flowing, you should lean back a little so the teat remains filled.

- Ensure they burb

If you notice any discomfort with them, stop the feeding. Hold them upright so they can wind a little. Once they finish feeding, hold them upright so they can burp. It's not advisable to lay them down immediately after eating. This can cause them to vomit or feel discomfort. Come on, even you, as an adult, aren't advised to lie down immediately after eating, and this rule also applies to babies.

- Prevent nipple confusion

Nipple confusion occurs when your baby is so used to feeding with a bottle that they avoid direct feeding. Allow your baby to practice feeding and breastfeeding. Overall, you should balance everything.

- The decision to accept a bottle is with your baby

Some baby easily accepts bottle, while others don't accept it all. So don't panic if your baby doesn't accept the bottle. While this can be disheartening, don't transfer your aggression to your baby. You can try different brands and see and perhaps they will find one that suits them perfectly.

- How to feed them with the bottle

Before you start feeding your baby with the bottle, first read the instructions that are written on the bottle pack. In short, give them the bottle and allow them to decide whether they want to feed on a bottle or not.

Splish Splash, Baby Bash: Grooming Your Little One with Finesse

It's necessary to give importance to grooming your baby with finesse so they will remain healthy and hygienic. There are also many ways you can achieve this. I will describe some of these ways, and the best part is that it's easy. You only need to incorporate most of these into your daily life. Here are they:

- Always give them neat hairstyles

You should always make sure your baby looks cute. Whether it's a boy or a girl, ensure you give them a nice hairstyle. If you can, do it yourself or take them to a professional. Initially, they won't have much hair to do so, and their scalp is delicate. So ensure they reach a certain stage before giving them this beautiful treatment. Some good ways to achieve this look include nicely combing their hair. If it's a girl, use some ribbons to pack the hair. Combing their hair regularly is beneficial too; it will lead to the growth of more hair. So, oil their hair constantly to keep it soft as well.

- Brush their teeth regularly

Clean your baby's mouth regularly. Here are some nice steps you can follow to do that.
- Grab a sterilized gauge, cotton, or any clean cloth and some water.
- Use a hand wash and thoroughly wash your hands.
- Wrap the piece around your finger and drip it inside the water to dampen it.
- Put the finger inside your baby's mouth gently, and wipe the upper and lower

gums. Do this process in the morning and night before they sleep.
- If they start developing teeth, you can change to a soft brush for children.
- To use a brush, wet it first, then put it in small toothpaste. If they are three years, you can use fluoridated toothpaste.

- You must give them a bath

You must bathe your baby every day in summer, then once in two days in winter. You can give them a sponge bath during chilly weather. Also, ensure to retain your baby's moisture by applying moisturizer or cream to their skin. There are many baby cream brands you can buy. Pediatricians usually recommend Cetaphil, especially if your baby has dry skin.

- Trim their nails

While trimming their nails, you should try to be extremely careful. I recommend you should immediately trim their nails after giving birth to them, do this when she is asleep because any slight mistake can lead to disaster. During your baby care shopping, you should purchase baby nail care products specifically designed for babies since they have tiny and soft hands. When cutting their fingernail, cut across the finger curve, and if you are cutting toenails, cut straight. You should also use a nail file to smoothen their edges. Your doctor may even recommend a nail file a few weeks after their bath.

- Clean their ear

Normally, wax covers your baby's ear; the wax contains healthy microbes that protect your baby's ear from infection. Here are some steps you can follow to clean your baby's ear:

- While cleaning the ear, be careful and stay away from the ear canal.
- Avoid using a cotton swab to clean the ear because it may push the wax inside the ear, leading to canal blockage.
- If you want to clean the ear and eliminate the blockage, make your baby lie on their side with the affected ear facing upward.
- Your pediatrician has probably prescribed an ear drop for you, so drop it inside the ear.
- Allow the baby to maintain the same position for ten minutes so the ear drop will loosen the wax gently.
- To encourage the drop to work on the ear canal, you can feed the baby; the sucking can also affect the ear.
- Clean the excess drops that are oozing out.
- The wax will come out after some time; use a cloth to clean it away.

- Ensure your baby smells nice

Most babies usually have a milk smell, so use a napkin to clean their mouth and neck after feeding them. Also, use diaper ointment after changing their diaper to avoid dirt smell.

- Massage their skin

Use safe oil to massage your baby's skin constantly, and always dress them in smart clothes. Avoid leaving them in their birth suit for a long time.

- Use bib

Always use a bib when feeding them. This will solve all the messy problems they will make and protect their dress from getting spoilt.

- Use footwear

At the early stage, use socks or soft footwear. As they age, use booties, slippers, sneakers, or any form of shoe of your choice.

- Always diaper them properly

This will help you prevent diaper mishaps and always carry extra diapers when going out.

Chapter 10: Soothing Techniques and Sleep Strategies

Sometimes, your baby will just start crying for reasons like hunger, illness, fatigue, and other related reasons. And there are also times that they will cry for no reason. This can be frustrating, I understand, but you need to cultivate patience to deal with them in this situation. Moreover, there are many soothing techniques and ways you can make your baby sleep.

In this chapter, I will discuss how you can make your baby and yourself sleep deeply. Also, I will talk about how you can make your little one safely sleep and survive the SIDS Scare. I will be doing justice to this chapter in three fascinating subsections. I'm sure you would find some value and amazing tips.

Let's get started.

Cry Me a River: Dad's Guide to Taming the Tiny Tears

Although dads are underappreciated almost everywhere in the world. However, you must let your baby feel your impact as you remain selfless. All being said, you can't sit and watch your little baby cry. You have to do something. In this subsection, I will share with you some incredible ways to come through for your baby in his moments of distress. Here you go:

- Find their pain

The first way to calm your baby is to find what bothers them. Singing for them will not stop them from feeling hungry, or changing their diaper will never stop them from crying if that is not what is worrying them. Rather it would help if you give them what they want. When you try all these, and you think nothing is wrong with them, then you can try some of these other techniques.

- Try the pinky

When you are not sure about the exact reason they are crying. Then stand up and wash your hand, then offer them your little finger to suck. If they didn't suck it, they would play with it. If it's teething that is bothering them, you can massage the area for them. It will make them stop crying. If this doesn't work, try this next step.

- Get them food

If your baby isn't on exclusive breastfeeding or they have to reach the stage of drinking water, give them water. It would help if you also bottle-fed them or called their mother to breastfeed them.

- Rock and swing

Most babies like movement, and is there any better way to give them this love aside from rock and swing? Once they start crying, you should lean on a chair and rocking them back and forth. You can also purchase a dual-purpose swing which will serve as a sedative and a form of exercise.

- Cut a rug

I suggest you throw your baby in the air and catch them, but believe me, your partner will never love this idea. So here is an alternative you should try. Hold them up your shoulder and let their hands wrap around your neck, gently dancing while rocking back and forth with one or two spins thrown in. If you feel like some noisy neighbors are cramping your style, draw the curtains and take their eyes off you. It would help if you also use your foot to tap the floor and try changing. Chant anything as long as it will match your dance beats. Once they start to keep quiet, you can lower your voice.

- Find embarrassing tune personal stunts

You can give them bodily functions, noises, and funny faces. Also, you can belly flop on top of any nearby cushion. Now you can use the physical gags you learned since childhood. Try BabyCenter's dad Mark Browne's trick, a father of two that turns cries into stares and usually giggles by placing something on his head and allowing it to fall. Then they will exclaim: Oh! It has fallen and laughed. Try this technique as much as you can until your baby stops crying.

- Rock and sing

Even though this might look embarrassing, you can sing any song for your child. I understand your voice might not be soothing but if it will at least make them stop crying, then that's a mission accomplished. But always respect your baby's taste. If you start singing and they increase their cry volume, kindly keep quiet before you damage their ear drum.

- Wear your baby

Put your baby in a front-loading sling. Between your body warmth, the beating of your heart, the rising and falling of your chest, and the gentle steps you take when walking. This can make them stop crying and even become curious about your heartbeat.

- Wait it out

Your partner may not find this likable, but at least it might be the best solution. If you try all these techniques mentioned above and none of them works. Then maybe your baby wants you to listen to them. You should place them on a comfortable surface and allow them to cry. Maybe they only want you to give them a listening ear, so allow them to cry as much as you can take it. If they keep quite fine, if not then pick them and try any of these methods again.

- Hand them over to their mom

The last step after trying everything and in avail is to hand them over to your partner. Maybe she has a way to soothe the baby.

Sleep or Sigh? Mastering the Art of Slumber for Your Baby (and Yourself)

Sleep is important for not only your baby but yourself too. It's one of the best ways to develop a healthy body and brain. Babies usually spend half of the time they used to sleep in a dream stage called Rapid Eye Movement to sleep. This stage is connected to brain activities like memory, nervous system function, and self-control. Babies don't have a night or day. Instead, they will sleep at their convenience and wake up when they wish. However, even though they are still tiny in their baby form, you can shape how they sleep in preparation for the future.

Below are little details you should engage in and pay attention to:

- Develop a rhythm

Babies usually spend most of their time sleeping, but they only spend an hour or so doing it in one go. They will sleep, wake up and go back to sleep again. Naturally, premature babies sleep more than babies born on their terms. At first, they won't have any specific sleeping pattern; they will sleep, wake up and feed, then return. But after some time, they will start remaining awake longer than before. They will assume a regular sleeping schedule as their brain and nervous system develop more and their stomach expand, holding more food.

Once your baby reaches three months, he will start a three times sleeping schedule, and they will sleep more at night. It might sound cliche, but getting enough sleep is important for the baby and their parents. In the first few months, you will feel exhausted, so without enough rest, you will fail to focus when doing many important things. Until you get into a new rhythm with your baby, it's best to set aside anything unnecessary and focus on resting whenever possible. By the time they reach 3 to 4 months, they will begin to sleep five hours in one go. So, always use this opportunity to rest too, unless you have something important to take care of.

- Have your baby sleep in your room

Unless their nursery is close to yours, have them sleep in your room when they are small. You can put a crib or bassinet near your bed for them. Your bed might be risky for them. When placed on a big bed, they may feel suffocated and trapped. Headboard slats and mattresses can trap them. If possible, have them stay in your room until they reach six months or even a year. This will also reduce the risk of sudden infant death syndrome. Another way you can protect them is by ensuring that they never get exposed to harmful air like cigarettes, smoke, and vaping. You can also get them a firm flat mattress.

- Encourage good sleeping habits

For the first few months, your baby will wake up in the middle of the night to feed, but it's never too early to teach them some good sleeping habits that will help you too.

- Follow a good bedtime routine: At first, your baby will set a sleeping routine for you, but you can also prepare them for the future by ensuring your bedroom always has a quiet and low-light atmosphere. Avoid playing with them at bedtime. Always keep your voice low and soothing to increase your interest in sleep. You

should follow the same sleeping routine as your other house members.
- Put your baby to bed drowsy but awake. Once you see signs of tiredness in them, such as when they start rubbing their eyes, take them to bed immediately. Also, remember to put your new baby on the back to sleep, except if your medical doctor says otherwise.
- Give your baby time to rest: Your baby may cry when sleepy. Therefore, you should make them rest on the bed, and allow some time before you check on them. Once they finish crying, they will eventually fall asleep. You can also swaddle them; some babies sleep fast when swaddled. Swaddling means wrapping them in a soft and cozy blanket and ensuring it's not tight.

- Use a pacifier: if your baby finds sleeping hard, a pacifier may do the trick. Research has even shown that using a pacifier on babies reduces the chances of sudden infant death syndrome. But if your baby is in their early stage, don't use a pacifier. Allow them to reach at least two to three months.

Generally, making your baby sleep and yourself it's something you will learn with them. Take your time and understand your baby's habits and ways of communication. This will allow you to help them to become better sleepers. If you have any concerns, talk to their healthcare provider.

Dreamland Delights: Snooze Safely and Survive the SIDS Scare

Sudden infant death syndrome (SIDS) has been responsible for numerous baby death. Although the rate has declined in recent years, it's still necessary for you to learn ways you can reduce the risk of this deadly syndrome.

- Don't allow your baby to sleep on their stomach

Allowing your baby to sleep on the back will reduce the risk of SIDS because they will access fresh air constantly compared to lying on their stomachs. If you must make them lie on their stomach, they should be on your lap where their faces are free, and they can also inhale easily. You may want to do it out of desperation because if you notice, you will see that babies tend to sleep more and longer when placed on their stomachs. But the satisfaction you will feel is for a short time, and while you are happy that they are sleeping, you are exposing them to the risk of dying early. But even though sleeping on stomachs is risky, you shouldn't worry much if your baby learns how to flip over and they turn and lay on their stomach. At this stage, they have grown, so once they feel the position is threatening their breathing, they will instantly flip back.

- Avoid side sleeping also

Another study has shown that placing a baby on the side is risky and can increase the chances of experiencing SIDS. A notable medical doctor, Dr. Moon, stated that "It's easier for an infant to roll onto their tummy from their side than from their back. And they may not yet have the skills to roll back in the other direction."

- Please don't put anything on their crib aside from a bedsheet

Putting things like blankets, comforters, or toys in your baby's crib can also increase the risk of SIDS because it can hinder your baby's breathing. Even soft or improperly fitted mattresses can also be a danger. So wait until they reach twelve months before you start stuffing their crib. If you are worried that they may develop a cold, especially if you are in chilly weather, then swaddle them. I've explained how to swaddle your baby safely earlier.

- Avoid using positioners or other baby gadgets for sleep

You may want to use stuff like breastfeeding or lounge pillows; please don't do that. It will also increase their risk of SIDS. Also, don't allow your baby to sleep on any surface except one approved by medical professionals, like a crib or bassinet. You should never use car seats, baby swings, or rock-and-play for sleep.

- Maintain a comfortable temperature in their nursery

Maintain a comfortable temperature in your baby's nursery. Too much cold or warmth can increase the risk too. Don't overheat them with swaddling or high room temperature. If you expose them to heat, it might be difficult for them to wake up.

- Avoid co-sleeping

It may tempt you to sleep with your baby on the same bed. Try and refrain from doing this. You might think you are giving them security, but you are sincerely exposing them to the risk. A pillow or blanket might suffocate your baby, and you may also roll over on them and cut an air supply. Their head can also be strangled when it gets entangled with a headboard or mattress.

If you want to cosleep, never put them on the same bed as you; rather, move their crib to your room and put it near your bed.

- Give enough room to your bed

To avoid SIDS, ensure your baby's crib is moderately spacious so they can turn and toss comfortably while sleeping. When your baby can't move properly, they may put themselves in a position that might endanger their lives. Put your baby with their hands above their head, and don't swaddle them too tight.

- Speak to your healthcare provider

The best way to prevent your baby from SIDS is to speak to their healthcare provider. They are the best people who advise you on how you can go about it and whether you need to take some measures. If you want to enroll your baby in a daycare, read all the daycare's precautions to protect children.

- Don't use anti-SIDS gadgets

Unless your baby is diagnosed with cardiac or respiratory disease, don't use any electronic breathing machine on your baby because it doesn't prevent SIDS. This may give you a misguided sense of security, but it's filled with risks and problems.

- Breastfeed your baby

Unless it's not safe for your partner to breastfeed your baby, allow your baby to have breasts more than formula. Babies who are breastfed are less likely to develop SIDS. Also, avoid exposing your baby to cigarettes smokes and other harmful air. Furthermore, avoid late-night nursing, be proactive, and make your baby sleep at the most appropriate time.

Additionally, if while feeding your baby you feel sleepy, lie down on the bed rather than a cushion or sofa; if you fall asleep while feeding them, return them to their crib once you wake up.

Conclusion: Mission Accomplished? Reflecting on Your Epic Journey as a First-Time Father

From Rookie to Rockstar: Celebrating Your Dad Superpowers

We have come so far in this book, and I'd love to express my heartfelt wish to you as a father, myself. Your unwavering dedication to ensuring that everything goes right, starting from the pregnancy procedure to the point of giving birth to your little bundle of joy, is highly commendable. As they say, the father is every girl's first love and every boy's first hero. I'm here to confirm that this statement is nothing short of the truth in all senses.

Your role has exceeded all expectations because whatever your baby becomes in the future, you are their first teacher. As a father, you have assumed the role of a leader and authority figure to your partner and children. Your influence is immeasurable, and your role is really special and important.

I estimate that you have learned a lot from these amazing books. You have graduated from someone with zero to nothing experience in taking care of children to someone that can cater to five or a dozen children comfortably — this is worth celebrating.

So what are the best ways to celebrate your superpowers? You can sit and reminisce with your partner while holding your adorable one; you can also take your partner out to celebrate; you can even simply sit and watch TV. There are countless ways you can celebrate these great achievements. Therefore, you can choose one that will be most memorable for both of you.

Parenthood Unplugged: Embracing the Hilarious Hiccups and Heartwarming Moments

Of course, there are many ways to embrace these hilarious hiccups and heartwarming moments. First, create a memento; whenever your baby does something adorable, snap those moments and keep it safe. This way, you will have a handmade and physical reminder; you can also sit and look at the pictures with your baby once they grow up. Also, find a safe box to keep some valuable things; these can be their first tooth after it falls off or anything funny and unique.

Bear in mind that you don't need any special occasion to celebrate. Every day should be Children's Day and Father's Day for your baby. Once in a while, after they grow up, cook something they love. You will be surprised at the extent it will put your family together.

To wrap everything up, tell everyone how proud you are as a dad; start with your baby's grandma and granddad, and let your baby know how proud you are of being their father. The big reason we celebrate with our children is to let them know how special they are. That's why in every celebration, food shouldn't be the priority — the memories you will make should be your focus.

Don't forget to drop your review. This will help other expectant and aspiring dads.

I wish you a wonderful experience in your journey to fatherhood.

Printed in Great Britain
by Amazon